Pep Talks for Mountain Movers

40 Daily Devotions for Parents
Healing Genetic Defects by Faith

Margaret Weishuhn

author of
God Heals Birth Defects - First Fruits

Forward by
Andy Hayner

DEDICATION

This book is dedicated to Team Avalanche, the parents and grandparents of faith. We are an elite army of parents and grandparents who are giving a God-sized report that directly conflicts with the diagnosis of our children and grandchildren. These doctor reports say that our children have incurable diagnosis like down syndrome and autism. We say that, with Jesus, we will have on earth what will be in Heaven for our children.

ACKNOWLEDGEMENTS

I want to thank Andy Hayner of Full Speed Impact Ministries for his excellent work as Editor in Chief of this devotional. His passion to advance the Kingdom of Heaven into the darkened arena of 'incurable' birth defects is rare and nothing less than the heart of our Savior for our children's freedom. He and his wife Tina, have made themselves available for countless hours of ministry and encouragement for many parents around the world, helping us to stand in faith. Thank you Andy and Tina.

I also want to thank Tim Cheatham and Linda Cameron for taking time to edit my writings. I am humbled and grateful for your long-suffering and exceptional skills with the English language!

I don't believe this book of encouragement would have made it without my loving husband, Will, and my technologically amazing daughter, Margaret Roland. It is awesome to journey this life of faith together!

I would also want to thank Tara Ashworth for contributing to many of the "Let's Worship Together" sections of this devotional. She is a worship leader in Canada who not only leads worship in her city, she also leads an organized global worship ministry for Team Avalanche.

CONTENTS

FOREWORD

BY

ANDY HAYNER

You are holding in your hand a precious jewel, a diamond in the Kingdom of God. This is a book that was forged in hidden places under a great deal of pressure. The truths and encouragement found in this book aren't "surface level" principles. They are life-or-death truths discovered in a knock-down, drag-out fight with the powers of hell.

God encourages every believer to follow the faith of those who inherit His promises "through faith **and perseverance**". We live in a day when most believers want to exercise their faith for a quick miracle in a moment of crisis, but will give up if it involves faith "and perseverance." These days, we like microwaves, not crockpots!

This book is a companion guide that builds upon the foundational teaching established in "God Heals Birth Defects - First Fruits." Whereas "God Heals Birth Defects" establishes the Biblical case with testimonies, in this follow up book you'll find the daily coaching, encouragement, and practical strategies you need to develop the perseverance you need to see your spiritual battle through to the victory that Jesus Christ has purchased for you. Part drill sergeant, part cheerleader, and great friend, Margaret has written this book to be a source of companionship for those who are walking lonely stretches of the road less traveled, the road of unyielding faith and obedience that will not yield to any work of the devil.

I've had the pleasure of knowing Margaret for several years and have watched God work through her to call the body of Christ to walk in their true identity and to set the captives free. She is a living rallying cry that we are to back down at nothing, even though it may seem "impossible." From our conversations, I can testify that she has not set out to "have a ministry" or to "be an author". She simply just hasn't forgotten where she came from. She remembers what it felt like to be told that birth defect and disease was "God's will". After she learned about healing in the atonement and the authority of the believer[1], she remembers what it felt like to feel all alone in the pathway of applying these truths in the realms of birth defect. Margaret has written this book because it's one way for her to "love her neighbor as herself." She's blazed a trail ahead of where most of us have walked, but she's not forgotten to do all she can to make the journey easier for others who may have a similar path to walk.

Although this book is written particularly for parents who are ministering healing to their children with a diagnosis of birth defect, the encouragement found here can easily be applied for those who are battling different health issues by faith.

Margaret is moving her mountain. In this book, she will help you do what it takes to move yours! You'll do it together.

---

[1] This book is written as an encouragement for people who have already come to this conviction. If you have not, please read, "God Heals Birth Defects - First Fruits" by Andy Hayner and Margaret Weishuhn

INTRODUCTION

"My child doesn't need to be healed from down syndrome. They are perfect just like they are. I don't want them any different". If these are your thoughts, then you are in the wrong book.

This book is for the sons and daughters of God who are aggressively and fervently enforcing the will of our Father who told us to pray for His will to BE DONE on earth as it is in Heaven. And we'll do it together!

We have already witnessed holes in hearts miraculously closing without surgery, faces changing appearances and becoming more normal, remarkable physical growth and developments, mental changes, many teachers and doctors witnessing the changes, even teeth appearing when the x-ray reports said it was impossible. We wrote a book about it!

We just haven't crossed the finish line yet for our children's manifested 100% healing. Most of us don't have strong support from our church, family, friends and communities, so we support each other. This book is a part of that support.

We may be small in number, but we're big in faith. This book is written to help bolster that faith. When the obstacles that we are overcoming appear daunting, part of our plan of overcoming them is to do it together.

My name is Margaret Weishuhn and "I am not ashamed of the gospel, for it is the power of God for salvation to everyone who believes, to the Jew first and also to the Greek. For in it the righteousness of God is revealed from faith for faith, as it is written, 'The righteous shall live by faith.' (Romans 1:16-17

ESV)

I have lost friends and made enemies all because I refuse to embrace the diagnosis of down syndrome as my child's identity. People's identities should not be that of disease when Jesus clearly bore all manner of sickness and disease at the whipping post. (Isaiah 53:4-5 & 1 Peter 2:24….make sure you look up the words in their original language for clear understanding!)

I am not alone. I am one in an army of many who are taking back what is rightfully their child's through the power and love of our God, Jehovah Rapha. We are busy setting our children free while much of the Church remains silent towards us. This silence is due solely to lack of understanding, which Jesus clearly taught would be the tool the enemy would use against us to steal the promises of God from us. (see Matthew 14:1-23, be sure to have your Strong's concordance handy to look up keywords in their original language).

This book is borne out of the Pep Talks I have shared with the valiant and faith filled parents and grandparents of Team Avalanche. No one can imagine the difficult and lonely path we have taken when we chose to take God at His Word. But God, our Father, has been good to us and brought us together from the corners of the world in order to stand in faith as a team, a family.

If you are not a member of Team Avalanche, you can take great courage that the path of the parents to minister healing to their children diagnosed with 'incurable' birth defects is well worn. We have paved a way for you to follow, though it is narrow and less traveled. We count ourselves especially blessed to be people of faith. Many say, "I'll believe it when I see it". Team Avalanche says, "We will see it **because** we believe it".

40 Daily Devotions for Parents

Healing Genetic Defects

by Faith

1

OUR BATTLE POSITION

Sometimes, in the clutter of life, ministering healing to our children can become burdensome and difficult. The time of day that I have ministered healing to my daughter, for the longest period of time, was at bedtime. I found that she would fall asleep in my arms as I rocked her and then I would go into fervent mode and minister healing to her. I would have to stir myself up just to pray because I was physically tired from the day. Though this time remained my longest set time of prayer in her presence for her, *my* presence wasn't always loving. I was solely ready for bed, and I was not looking forward to missing the much needed sleep.

I think my weariness came from not knowing my exact position for the mission.

I recently inquired of the Lord intensely for a deeper understanding regarding this long battle for my child's freedom from defect. My daughter's healing has, up until this point, seemed to be as slow as a snail. I've been ministering healing successfully with various other diseases, but as far as my daughter is concerned, her transformation seems to have taken the long route.

Jesus never halfway healed anyone, and He certainly is not going to start now.

I read in the book of Joshua where God told Joshua to point his sword (spear) towards the enemy's walled city during a battle to remove an enemy fortress that was on Israel's Promised Land. God told him that as long as that sword was pointing towards the enemy's city that he would defeat the enemy for them. Joshua did as he was instructed and they won this battle. They showed up for the battle, but God won it for them. They weren't ignorant to the protection and power of their God, nor did they doubt His Word.

This position in battle took all the pressure off of Joshua. Now when I pray for my child's freedom from birth defect, I actually picture myself in this battle scene as if I were in Joshua's position. I don't let up my position to stand firm on the truth, direct my sword (the Word of God) towards the problem. Because of this I know, without a shadow of a doubt, that God is removing the obstacles that stand in the way of my child manifesting complete healing.

So here is our mission position: We stand with our mouths filled with the promises of God for our children. We aim our swords, God's Word, towards the targets and release the Word! We do it in faith. Unbelief is treason and punishable by the death of our children's destinies. Behold our God who performs His word. He does the work. We show up on the battlefield with our shields of faith and sword of the Word and our God does the Work.

To your Battle Position, Mighty soldier of valor!

We'll do it together!

GOD SPEAKS:

"For you equipped me with strength for the battle; you made those who rise against me sink under me." (Psalm 18:39 ESV)

"The eyes of the LORD are toward the righteous and his ears toward their cry. The face of the LORD is against those who do evil, to cut off the memory of them from the earth. When the righteous cry for help, the LORD hears and delivers them out of all their troubles. The LORD is near to the brokenhearted and saves the crushed in spirit. Many are the afflictions of the righteous, but the LORD delivers him out of them all." (Psalm 34:15-19 ESV)

"Behold, I have given you authority to tread on serpents and scorpions, and over all the power of the enemy, and nothing shall hurt you." (Luke 10:19 ESV)

LET'S WORSHIP TOGETHER

'Waging War', sung and written by Cece Winans

NOTE: The YouTube video playlist for the Worship Songs included in this devotional is found at **FullSpeedImpact.com under the Team Avalanche tab.**

Anoint my head anoint my feet, Send your angels raining down, Here on the battle ground, For your glory, We're taking territory, Fighting unseen enemies, Like never before, We're Waging War
[Bridge:]

I'm tired of principalities, Messing with me, (Waging war) I'm tired of the devil, Stealing from me, (Waging war) I promise he won't get, One more thing (Waging war) I'm taking it back, Taking territory (Waging war), I'm ready for the battle, I'm ready to win, (Waging war) My weapon of power, He lives within (Waging war)

I can't be defeated. The enemy gotta flee (waging war) I'm taking it back, Taking territory, Going into battle, Going into battle, Be my sword, Be my shield, As we claim the victory, Over the enemy, In your name, You rule and reign, Never being defeated Anymore, We're waging war

[Bridge]
Send your fire, Send your fire

[Bridge 2:]
Fire by night, Cloud by day, A strong tower, Send the latter rain, Lion of Judah, Lord, God, Mighty In battle, Since you did, It back then, We know you'll do, It again, We're going into battle, We're going into battle, Waging war

2

BEFORE YOU BOW THE KNEE TO UNGODLY SORROW, TRY THIS!

You know that sadness that sometimes tries to overtake us that has the ability to fill our hearts and results in crying and deep sorrow? Maybe you don't deal with that, but I have. I used to cry every day, kneeling and covering my head so my children could not hear my sobs and words to God. I would choke on my words to God and where I was kneeling would be dampened with my tears and stained with mascara...you understand the scene? Well, here is the challenge if this is something that you go thru: if your emotions ever try to overwhelm your productivity and energy and clarity, here is what I challenge you with!

When the waters of sorrow try to overtake you do this: Stand up on your feet and stand tall. Hold your head up and go to a room where you can have privacy. Deny the tears and don't slouch.

Here is what I want us to say: "Father, You are not a man that you should lie. You are the same yesterday today and forever. You charged us to pray your will be done on earth as it is in Heaven. You said that by the stripes of Jesus my child WAS healed. You gave me authority over all the powers of the enemy. Everything you gave Jesus you gave to me as well.

I'm going to use his name, his authority, your promises, your will and your word right now. I expect the truth to manifest in my child from the top of their head to the tip of their toes. You are Jehovah Rapha, the God who heals. It is your nature to heal. It is your will and your promise that healing is my child's inheritance. Thank you. Thank you for being trustworthy. Thank you for performing your Word. Thank you for healing my child. Thank you that the truth is manifesting in my child and cannot be stopped until every cell and every bit of development is lined up with the truth."

Go put some water on to boil and find some tea. Make yourself a cup of tea and don't slouch. You are in a good place because you are trusting God. Even if it appears that no one is standing with you, you are not alone. Even if your family thinks you've gone off the deep end, you will not turn away from trusting in our God and His promises!

GOD SPEAKS:
"I can do all things through him who strengthens me."
(Philippians 4:13 ESV)

"Fear not, for I am with you, be not dismayed, for I am your God; I will strengthen you, I will help you, I will uphold you with my righteous right hand." (Isaiah 41:10-11 ESV)

LET'S WORSHIP TOGETHER!

<u>Worthy Of It All, sung and written by; David Brymer</u>
All the saints and angels bow before Your throne
All the elders cast their crowns before the Lamb of God and sing
You are worthy of it all, You are worthy of it all,
For from You are all things, And to You are all things,
You deserve the glory
Day and night, night and day, let incense arise
Day and night, night and day, let incense arise
Day and night, night and day, let incense arise
Day and night, night and day, let incense arise

3

WORTHY OF OUR TRUST

As I knelt by my daughter's bed to pray for her tonight, my prayers took a different turn. As I spoke softly to the Holy Spirit, I was keenly aware of His presence. I began to thank the Lord for healing my child. I thanked him for healing her brain, her breathing, her hair, her chromosomes and speech. It was a genuine faith filled conversation with the Lord. Now, I'm not going to stop laying hands on her, (Mark 16:18), and commanding her body to do what it should be doing or speaking life to her brain and body. I will do everything that Jesus modeled for us.

I've known that my daughter would be completely healed from down syndrome here on earth, but tonight my faith went to a new level. My thankfulness for her wholeness was based on HIS faithfulness. I kept telling him over and over, "I trust you, I trust you" and I meant it.

What an incredibly awesome place to be in! To be a people who have faith in their God! That's us!

Today's assignment: let's repeatedly thank our Lord and Savior, Jesus, for healing our children. We'll do this together!

GOD SPEAKS:

"Bless the LORD, O my soul, and all that is within me, bless his holy name! Bless the LORD, O my soul, and forget not all his benefits, who forgives all your iniquity, who heals all your diseases, who redeems your life from the pit, who crowns you with steadfast love and mercy, who satisfies you with good so that your youth is renewed like the eagles." (Psalm 103:1-5 ESV)

LET'S WORSHIP TOGETHER!

"Good Good Father", Chris Tomlinson. Sung by; Tara Ashworth

Oh, I've heard a thousand stories of what they think you're like but I've heard the tender whisper of love in the dead of night
You tell me that you're pleased and that I'm never alone
You're a Good, Good Father
It's who you are, It's who you are, It's who you are
and I'm loved by you It's who I am, It's who I am, It's who I am
I've seen many searching for answers far and wide
But I know we're all searching for answers only you provide
Because you know just what we need before we say a word
You're a Good, Good Father It's who you are, It's who you are,
It's who you are and I'm loved by you It's who I am, It's who I am, It's who I am
You're a Good, Good Father It's who you are, It's who you are,
It's who you are and I'm loved by you
It's who I am, It's who I am, It's who I am
You are perfect in all of your ways, You are perfect in all of your ways
You are perfect in all of your ways to us, You are perfect in all of your ways
You are perfect in all of your ways, You are perfect in all of your ways to us
OH it's Love so undeniable I, I can hardly speak
Peace so Unexplainable I, I can hardly think
As you call me deeper still, as you call me deeper still

As you call me deeper still into love love love
You're a Good, Good Father It's who you are, It's who you are,
It's who you are and I'm loved by you
It's who I am, It's who I am, It's who I am

4

PERSISTENCE

Persistence = (definition) "firm or obstinate continuance in a course of action in spite of difficulty or opposition."

If it is yours rightfully yours, purchased with flesh and blood, then sorrow and grief are not the emotions that will aid you. Trusting in our Great and Mighty God with downright determination, tenacity, and stubborn, relentless & stalwart belief **will** aid you! Our God is "not a man that he should lie." (Numbers 23:19) His very nature is to set things right and bring order out of chaos.

Stand on this truth. Shout this truth. Whisper this truth. Dance this truth. Sleep on the pillow of victory in this truth. Take a permanent vacation from the deep sorrow and griefs because of this very truth. Do not, I repeat, do not let your thoughts be fruitful if they contradict the truth.

Any victory I have had in setting people free from disease and sickness was when I went in, fixed on the outcome before I even met them, knowing that they were already healed, (see 1 Peter 2:24) knowing that any devil or disease would bow the knee to the name of Jesus and the truth of the Word of God, before I arrived.

And I did not take no for an answer.

My child, and your child, are in process of manifesting the truth of the scars on Jesus back. Let's do this freedom march with class! Let's do it in a fashion that will bring honor to our king and God! Let's do it with a smile on our faces that spills out from a glad heart that is trusting our God; and let's not step away from this victorious battlefield that will surely echo throughout history shouting, "'yes', the sons of God manifested and 'yes' their children were indeed healed down to the very "DNA".

We'll be able to say, 'We did it together'!"

GOD SPEAKS

"For the creation waits with eager longing for the revealing of the sons of God." (Romans 8:19 ESV)

"You are my witnesses," declares the LORD, and my servant whom I have chosen, that you may know and believe me and understand that I am he. Before me no god was formed, nor shall there be any after me. I, I am the LORD, and besides me there is no savior. I declared and saved and proclaimed, when there was no strange god among you; and you are my witnesses," declares the LORD, "and I am God." (Isaiah 43:10-12 ESV)

LET'S WORSHIP TOGETHER!

<u>Not for a Moment, sung by; Meredith Andrews</u>
You were reaching through the storm, Walking on the water
Even when I could not see In the middle of it all, When I thought You
were a thousand miles away, Not for a moment did You forsake me, Not
for a moment did You forsake me

After all You are constant. After all You are only good. After all You are
sovereign, Not for a moment will You forsake me Not for a moment will
You forsake me

You were singing in the dark, Whispering Your promise, Even when I
could not hear, I was held in Your arms, Carried for a thousand miles to
show, Not for a moment did You forsake me

And every step every breath you are there, Every tear every cry every prayer,
In my hurt at my worst, When my world falls down, Not for a moment
will You forsake me, Even in the dark, Even when it's hard, You will
never leave me, After all

Not for a moment will You forsake me

5

THE KITCHEN TIMER FAST

For those seemingly difficult and endless days

Many years ago, I started doing this and want to share the wisdom in it if you are having difficult and long days. Every hour my kitchen timer was set and every hour on the hour when it went off, I would go into the kitchen, get on my knees, sometimes prostrate myself on the kitchen floor, and talk to Jesus. My children, who were small at the time, would prostrate themselves beside me and mimic me. I didn't care, I needed help and I recognized where my help came from. It worked.

The deception, many times, is thinking that we are alone in our daily battle to "be strong and courageous", trusting our God to fulfill His promises. He promised that He would never leave us. He promised that He was the God who heals all our diseases. He promised us that Jesus bore all manner of sickness and disease. He promised us that He was our deliverer, savior and ever present help. He promised us that He is not a man that lies. He promised that he is the same yesterday today and forever.

We will be brave and trust him for He is worthy of our trust. He never goes back on His Word and we will do this together! Now… go get your timer!

GOD SPEAKS:

"But blessed is the one who trusts in the Lord, whose confidence is in him. They will be like a tree planted by the water that sends out its roots by the stream. It does not fear when heat comes; its leaves are always green. It has no worries in a year of drought and never fails to bear fruit." (Jeremiah 17:7-8 ESV)

"Let us hold fast the confession of our hope without wavering, for he who promised is faithful". (Hebrews 10:23ESV)

LET'S WORSHIP TOGETHER!
'You Make Me Brave', Amanda Cook & Bethel Music
I stand before You now, The greatness of your renown I have heard of the majesty and wonder of you, King of Heaven, in humility, I bow

As Your love, in wave after wave Crashes over me, crashes over me For You are for us You are not against us Champion of Heaven You made a way for all to enter in

I have heard You calling my name I have heard the song of love that You sing, So I will let You draw me out beyond the shore Into Your grace Your grace

You make me brave, You make me brave, You call me out beyond the shore into the waves, You make me brave, You make me brave, No fear can hinder now the love that made a way

You make me brave, You make me brave, You call me out beyond the shore into the waves, You make me brave, You make me brave, No fear can hinder now the promises you made, You make me brave, You make me brave, No fear can hinder now the love that made a way

6
IF I WERE THE ENEMY

If I were the enemy and I saw that you had found the truth of what Jesus had done for your child diagnosed with down syndrome or any other incurable birth defect; and I saw that your lips said you believed this truth, but your daily responses told a different story...then I would give you a run for your money. I wouldn't just up and leave you alone just because your lips said one thing when your actions said something completely different.

If I were the enemy, I would observe you to see if you actually believed what you said. If you were the weak one, tossed to and fro with a contradicting lifestyle and doctrine, then you would be my easy and obvious target. I'd focus on you until you gave up and quit.

When you are worshipping God in your home, when no person can see you, when you are praying for others as you go along life's path, when you are thanking God for what he has done for your child before you can actually see the change, you are establishing a reputation in the spiritual realm.

Without words, these things demonstrate that you believe what you say you believe. And these things reflect faith, which is the substance that overcomes the world. It is the only ingredient that pleases God and moves mountains.

God's will be done in our lives this day on earth as it is in Heaven. May we both dance in advance as we journey this freedom march for our children!
We can take encouragement from what God told the Israelites. I believe He is saying this to us this day:

GOD SPEAKS:

"Be strong and courageous, do not be afraid or tremble at them, for the LORD your God is the one who goes with you He will not fail you or forsake you." Then Moses called to Joshua and said to him in the sight of all Israel, "Be strong and courageous, for you shall go with this people into the land which the LORD has sworn to their fathers to give them, and you shall give it to them as an inheritance. "The LORD is the one who goes ahead of you; He will be with you He will not fail you or forsake you. Do not fear or be dismayed."(Deuteronomy 31:6-8)

LET'S WORSHIP TOGETHER!
Our God Reigns Here-John Waller

Spirit of death you have no place here, I command you to leave in Jesus' name, Spirit of fear you have no place here I command you to leave in Jesus' name, You're not welcome here so go, just go

Spirit of death you have no place here, I command you to leave in Jesus' name, Envy and jealousy you have no place here, I command you to leave in Jesus' name, Go back from whence you came

'Cause our God reigns here, our God reigns here, We claim this ground in Jesus' name, 'Cause our God reigns, Our God reigns here, our God reigns here, The battle's won, have no fear, 'Cause God reigns here, He reigns here our God

Anger and rage, guilt and shame, I command you to leave in Jesus' name, Depression, anxiety, addiction, infirmity, I command you to leave in Jesus' name, Oh, go back from whence you came

'Cause our God reigns here, our God reigns here We claim this ground in Jesus' name image: 'Cause our God reigns

Our God reigns here, our God reigns here. The battle's won, have no fear 'Cause God reigns here, There's no doubt He has overcome the world, And God reigns here, There's no doubt He has overcome the world

'Cause our God reigns here, our God reigns here, We claim this ground in Jesus' name, 'Cause our God reigns

Our God reigns here, our God reigns here, The battle's won, have no fear, The battle's won, have no fear, The battle's won, have no fear, 'Cause God reigns here

There's no doubt He has overcome the world, And God reigns here, There's no doubt He has overcome the world, And our God reigns.

7

IF YOU CAN'T SAY ANYTHING GOOD, DON'T SAY ANYTHING AT ALL

That's it! That's my victory tip of the day. "If you can't say anything good, don't say anything at all." I challenge you to this! Are you up for the challenge? Let's do it together. Game on!

Here is an excellent example of two men of God who met this challenge head on and passed the test. Joshua and Caleb gave a report that was acceptable to the Lord when spying on their promised land. They were allowed to enter the land.

The other ten spies were not allowed to enter the promised land because they gave the facts when reporting their findings. God called their report an 'evil report'.

You are called to have the same mindset that Joshua and Caleb had when they were faced with insurmountable odds, save their God.

We trust our God to do the work and we do not waver from our battle position of stalwart, fervent and immovable faith. We wield our swords, the unfailing Word of God, every step of the way knowing that His word will not return void.

Read for yourself the account of Caleb and Joshua's report. It included God as their victorious resource and this enabled them to enter the Promised Land. (Numbers 13:25-33, 14:1-38 ESV)

GOD SPEAKS:

"For the righteous will never be moved; he will be remembered forever. He is not afraid of bad news; his heart is firm, trusting in the LORD." (Psalm 112:6-7 ESV)

Grab a cup of tea or coffee and crank up the praise music!

LET'S WORSHIP TOGETHER!

The Maker-Chris August

I see You in the sunrise, I see You in the rain, I see You in the laughter, I feel You through the pain, Everything that You have made is beautiful, Oh, my God, I can't believe my eyes, But in all of this to think that You would think of me, Makes my heart come alive.

[Chorus:]
Your love is like a mighty fire deep inside my bones
I feel like I could climb a thousand mountains all at once
And I never have to wonder if somebody cares for me
I love the Maker and the Maker loves me

I see You, You are creation, I see the grandness of Your majesty, The universe is singing all Your glory, I can't believe You live inside of me, Everything that You have made is beautiful, Oh, my God, I can't believe my eyes, But in all of this to think that You would think of me, Makes my heart come alive
[Chorus]
More than just some words upon a page, You've shown me in a million ways, But there is one that stands above them all. Hands of creation on a cross

8
FOG OF WAR

The fog of war is 'confusion caused by the chaos of war or battle: (ex.) he argues that the fog of war clouded everyone's judgment'. (Oxford Dictionary)

It can happen anywhere and the enemy usually doesn't have to orchestrate too much to get our minds distracted from the truth and on to the hard and difficult report of the facts. The enemy can use a stranger, a family member, a friend, a therapist and even your own mind to be distracted by thoughts of sorrow, defeat and facts. Remember, we are people of faith, and truth trumps fact every time.'

Here is where your participation is paramount in overcoming the Fog of War on this battlefield of freeing our children. You have to rely on the Holy Spirit to alert you to the fog of war when it occurs in your day. Ask Him to give you discernment to know when this is happening.

Your will to win in the 'fog of war' includes and is not limited to <u>taking charge of your thoughts</u>. You **can** do this because you have Christ Jesus! (see Philippians 4:13)

We'll do it together!

GOD SPEAKS:

"For though we walk in the flesh, we are not waging war according to the flesh. For the weapons of our warfare are not of the flesh but have divine power to destroy strongholds. We destroy arguments and every lofty opinion raised against the knowledge of God, and take every thought captive to obey Christ, being ready to punish every disobedience, when your obedience is complete." (2 Corinthians 10:3-6 ESV)

"You keep him in perfect peace, whose mind is stayed on you, because he trusts in you. Trust in the LORD forever, for the LORD GOD is an everlasting rock." (Isaiah 26:3-4)

LET'S WORSHIP TOGETHER!

Only King Forever- Elevation Worship.
Sung by; Tara Ashworth

Our God a firm foundation
Our rock, the only solid ground
As nations rise and fall
Kingdoms once strong now shaken
But we trust forever in Your Name
The Name of Jesus
We trust the Name of Jesus
You are the only King forever
Almighty God we lift You higher
You are the only King forever
Forevermore, You are victorious
Unmatched in all Your wisdom
In love and justice You will reign
And every knee will bow
We bring our expectations
Our hope is anchored in Your Name
The Name of Jesus
Oh, we trust the Name of Jesus
You are the only King forever
Almighty God we lift You higher
You are the only King forever
Forevermore, You are victorious
We lift our banner high
We lift the Name of Jesus
From age to age You reign
Your kingdom has no end
You are the only King forever
Almighty God we lift You higher
You are the only King forever
Forevermore, You are victorious

9

TWO REASONS

YOU ARE NOT GOING TO QUIT

#1 YOU ARE NOT GOING TO QUIT BECAUSE IT'S THE TRUTH.
Jesus paid for your child's healing in full at the whipping post.
The Word of God is the Word of God.
It's the truth.

#2 YOU ARE NOT GOING TO QUIT BECAUSE YOU ARE GOING TO LOVE YOUR NEIGHBOR AS YOURSELF
Your child is as close to your neighbor as you can get.
It's the right thing to do.

You would want someone to do it for you. God has placed you in the company of *valor*, parents around the world are standing beside you.

Put every thought , every reason, every logic in your mind that is coming against the truth of the whipping post and throw those thoughts down and trample on them.2 Corinthians 10:5 "Casting down every imagination (Greek word meaning=reason & logic) and everything that exalts itself against the knowledge of God and take captive every thought to the obedience of Christ"

Defeat is not an option. Quitting is not in your vocabulary.

GOD SPEAKS:

'Though I walk in the midst of trouble, you preserve my life; you stretch out your hand against the wrath of my enemies, and your right hand delivers me. The LORD will fulfill his purpose for me; your steadfast love, O LORD, endures forever.' (Psalm 138:7-8 ESV)

Forever, O LORD, your word is firmly fixed in the heavens. Your faithfulness endures to all generations; you have established the earth, and it stands fast. By your appointment they stand this day, for all things are your servants. If your law had not been my delight, I would have perished in my affliction. I will never forget your precepts, for by them you have given me life.' (Psalm 119:89-93 ESV)

LET'S WORSHIP TOGETHER!

'Every Praise' Hezekiah Walker

Every praise is to our God. Every word of worship with one accord Every praise every praise is to our God. Sing hallelujah to our God, Glory hallelujah is due our God.

Every praise every praise is to our God. Every praise is to our God. Every word of worship with one accord. Every praise every praise is to our God. Sing hallelujah to our God. Glory hallelujah is due our God Every praise every praise is to our God. Every praise is to our God. Every word of worship with one accord. Every praise every praise is to our God.

Sing hallelujah to our God, Glory hallelujah is due our God, Every praise every praise is to our God, Every praise is to our God. Every word of worship with one accord, Every praise every praise is to our God. Sing hallelujah to our God, Glory hallelujah is due our God, Every praise every praise is to our God.

God my Savior, God my Healer, God my Deliverer, Yes He is, yes He is, God my Savior, God my Healer, God my Deliverer, Yes He is, yes He is, God my Savior, God my Healer, God my Deliverer

Yes He is, yes He is, yes He is, yes He is, Yes He is, yes He is, yes He is, yes He is

Every praise is to our God., Every word of worship with one accord, Every praise, every praise, every praise, every praise, Every praise, every praise, every praise, every praise, Every praise, every praise, every praise, every praise,

---

33

All of my worship, every praise, Every praise, every praise, When you see me dancing, every praise, Every praise, every praise, When you see me shoutin', every praise Every praise, every praise, every praise, every praise Every praise, every praise, to our God, Is to our God, Every praise is to our God.

10

PUT YOUR FEET IN THE WATER!

When the Israelites were crossing over from the desert that they had wandered in for forty years on the way to their Promised Land, God gave Joshua specific instructions on how to get across the obstacle that was in front of them. God instructed Joshua to have the Priests go first and put their feet into the river that stood between the Israelites and their promise. At that time God's Spirit was inside the Ark of the Covenant which the Priests were ordained to physically carry on this journey to their Promise.

They had to make the first move before the miraculous occurred. They took the presence of God with them on their shoulders and after they stepped into the Jordan River, the waters parted.

Like the Levitical Priests, we too carry the presence of God on earth as Christians, only He is inside of us. We are sort of like walking-talking Arks of the Covenant!

Our job is to go forward in faith knowing that if God said it is ours to possess, then that is how it is going to be. He is in us and with us every step of the way.

GOD SPEAKS:

"The Lord said to Joshua, 'Today I will begin to exalt you in the sight of all Israel, that they may know that, as I was with Moses, so I will be with you. And as for you, command the priests who bear the ark of the covenant, When you come to the brink of the waters of the Jordan, you shall stand still in the Jordan' So when the people set out from their tents to pass over the Jordan with the priests bearing the ark of the covenant before the people, and as soon as those bearing the ark had come as far as the Jordan, and the feet of the priests bearing the ark were dipped in the brink of the water the waters coming down from above stood and rose up in a heap very far away, at Adam, the city that is beside Zarethan, and those flowing down toward the Sea of the Arabah, the Salt Sea, were completely cut off. And the people passed over opposite Jericho. Now the priests bearing the ark of the covenant of the Lord stood firmly on dry ground in the midst of the Jordan, and all Israel was passing over on dry ground until all the nation finished passing over the Jordan." (Joshua 3:7-8,4:14-17)

LET'S WORSHIP TOGETHER!

'Oceans', Hillsong Uniteed

You call me out upon the waters, The great unknown where feet may fail,
and there I find You in the mystery, in oceans deep, My faith will stand
And I will call upon Your name, And keep my eyes above the waves,
When oceans rise, My soul will rest in Your embrace
For I am Yours and You are mine

Your grace abounds in deepest waters, Your sovereign hand
Will be my guide, Where feet may fail and fear surrounds me
You've never failed and You won't start now
So I will call upon Your name,

And keep my eyes above the waves, When oceans rise, My soul will rest in
Your embrace, For I am Yours and You are mine

Spirit lead me where my trust is without borders, Let me walk upon the
waters, Wherever You would call me, Take me deeper than my feet could
ever wander, And my faith will be made stronger, In the presence of my
Savior,

Spirit lead me where my trust is without borders, Let me walk upon the
waters, Wherever You would call me, Take me deeper than my feet could
ever wander, And my faith will be made stronger, In the presence of my
Savior, Spirit lead me where my trust is without borders, Let me walk
upon the waters, Wherever You would call me, Take me deeper than my
feet could ever wander,

And my faith will be made stronger, In the presence of my Savior, Spirit
lead me where my trust is without borders
Let me walk upon the waters, Wherever You would call me
Take me deeper than my feet could ever wander, And my faith will be
made stronger, In the presence of my Savior,

Oh Jesus yeah, my God, I will call upon Your Name, Keep my eyes above the waves, My soul will rest in Your embrace
I am Yours and You are mine.

11

DO YOU FEEL LIKE YOU ARE ON THE LEDGE?

DON'T JUMP!

Here is how we handle days like these:

Recognize this feeling of despair for what it is first of all. This is a <u>spiritual attack</u> from the enemy to convince you to give up and quit.

You need to have a prayer buddy, someone who will love your child as their own and pray for you, your child, and your family. You need someone who will partner with you, a highly trained swordsmen who will know how to get the enemy off of you thru prayer! Don't have one? Ask the Holy Spirit to provide one for you. Count on Him to provide this.

More importantly, control what you are listening to, including thoughts that don't line up with the victory we firmly have in Christ Jesus. Replace your thoughts with the Word of God. For goodness sakes, do your part by turning off the thoughts that are bringing you down the path of wrong thinking.

We'll do it together!

GOD SPEAKS:

"You keep him in perfect peace whose mind is stayed on you, because he trusts in you." (Isaiah 26:3)

LET'S WORSHIP TOGETHER!

'I Call You Faithful', Donnie McClurkin

I call You holy, Your name is holy You are so holy to me
I call You holy, Your name is holy Holy You are and holy You'll be

I call You holy, Your name is holy, You are so holy to me, I call You holy,
Your name is holy, Holy You are and holy You'll be Yeah, yeah, yeah,
yeah, yeah, yeah

I call You righteous, Your name is righteous, You are so righteous to me, I
call You righteous, Your name is righteous, Righteous You are and
righteous You'll be Yeah, yeah, yeah, yeah, yeah, yeah

I call You awesome, Your name is awesome, You are so awesome to me, I
call You awesome, Your name is awesome, Awesome You are and
awesome You'll be Yeah, yeah, yeah, yeah, yeah, yeah

I call You faithful, Your name is faithful, You are so faithful to me, I call
You faithful, Your name is faithful, Faithful You are and faithful You'll
be Yeah, yeah, yeah, yeah, yeah, yeah

I call You healer, Your name is healer. You are the healer to me, I call
You healer, Your name is healer, Healer You are and healer You'll be
Yeah, yeah, yeah, yeah, yeah, yeah

I call You savior, Your name is savior, You are the savior to me, somebody
say, I call You savior, Your name is savior, Savior You are and savior
You'll be Yeah, yeah, yeah, yeah, yeah, yeah

I call You all that, Your name is all that, You have been all that to me I
call You all that, Your name is all that, All that You are and all that
You'll be, Yeah, yeah, yeah, yeah, yeah, yeah

12

"I AM HAVING A DIFFICULT TIME
LOOKING AT MY CHILD
AND NOT BEING SAD"

"I do not like the way my child looks. It grieves me deeply. Is something wrong with me?" I've been asked this question many times.

If someone were to come into your home and break all of your mirrors & lamps, rip your upholstery furniture to shreds and write graffiti all over your walls, would you be o.k. with that? Of course not! Until justice was served and your house was back the way it should be, you are going to be reminded of the thievery and it would probably affect your demeanor.

It is the same way with our children. It is no longer acceptable to have symptoms of defect when we decide to believe God's words to us about healing. We like to think of this time of healing as an exciting and expecting time! A time to watch our children blossom into the children (or adults) that God desires them to be. It's not easy to remain in faith when you are believing for something that you cannot see, so surround yourself with faith filled Believers and ask them to walk the journey of healing with you.

GOD SPEAKS:

"For all the promises of God find their Yes in him. That is why it is through him that we utter our Amen to God for his glory."
(2 Corinthians 1:20 ESV)

LET'S WORSHIP TOGETHER!

'Glorious Unfolding', Steven Curtis Chapman

Lay your head down tonight, Take a rest from the fight, Don't try to figure it out, Just listen to what I'm whispering to your heart, 'Cause I know this is not, Anything like you thought, The story of your life was gonna be, And it feels like the end has started closing in on you, But it's just not true

*There's so much of the story that's still yet to unfold
And this is going to be a glorious unfolding
Just you wait and see and you will be amazed
You've just got to believe the story is so far from over
So hold on to every promise God has made to us
And watch this glorious unfolding*

*God's plan from the start, For this world and your heart
Has been to show His glory and His grace, Forever revealing the depth and the beauty of His unfailing Love, And the story has only begun*

And this is going to be a glorious unfolding, Just you wait and see and you will be amazed, We've just got to believe the story is so far from over, So hold on to every promise God has made to us, And watch this glorious unfolding

We were made to run through fields of forever, Singing songs to our Savior and King, So let us remember this life we're living, Is just the beginning of the beginning, Of this glorious unfolding

We will watch and see and we will be amazed, If we just keep on believing the story is so far from over, And hold on to every promise God has made to us, We'll see the glorious unfolding, Just watch and see (unfolding), This is just the beginning of the beginning (unfolding)

13

WE ARE AN ARMY OF PARENTS LETHAL TO THE KINGDOM OF DARKNESS. WE ARE THE SONS AND DAUGHTERS OF GOD.

We all want our children to be 100% defect free. We all know that Jesus paid for this in full. We all know that we have the capacity to minister healing to our children and our neighbor's child. What we do not want is to put our faith in man for our child's healing— any man other than Jesus.

I did my time searching the globe looking for someone, other than my husband and myself, to lay hands or pray for my child and get her healed, until I understood who I was in Christ Jesus and what I carried.

Having someone like Andy Hayner or Curry Blake pray for our children is super! However, they have the same spirit that raised Christ Jesus from the dead that we have inside of us. Their results are coming because they understand who they are in Christ Jesus.

We can be grateful for the help we receive in bringing God's will to pass in our children; but let's not miss what the Father wants us to have: a renewed mind as to who we are in Christ Jesus. This should be our weekly goal, to gain better understanding as to who we are in Christ Jesus. When our children are manifesting completely healed bodies, we must be able to explain to others (who will ask us no doubt) the "how" &"why". God wants us to take back the planet and make it look like it should on earth as it is in Heaven.

WE are the sons and daughters of God that the earth has been groaning in expectation of for centuries and centuries. We are talked about in the Romans 8:19

Let's not waste a day without renewing our minds as to who we truly are IN Christ Jesus.

GOD SPEAKS:

"The natural person does not accept the things of the Spirit of God, for they are folly to him, and he is not able to understand them because they are spiritually discerned. The spiritual person judges all things, but is himself to be judged by no one. "For who has understood the mind of the Lord so as to instruct him?" But we have the mind of Christ." (1 Corinthians 2:14-16 ESV)

LET'S WORSHIP TOGETHER!

"Vicotor's Crown"- Darlene Zschech

Sung by Tara Ashworth

You are always fighting for us
Heaven's angels all around
My delight is found in knowing
That You wear the Victor's crown
You're my help and my defender
You're my Saviour and my friend
By Your grace I live and breathe
To worship You
At the mention of Your greatness
In Your Name I will bow down
In Your presence fear is silent
For You wear the Victor's crown
Let Your glory fill this temple
Let Your power overflow
By Your grace I live and breathe
To worship You
Hallelujah
You have overcome
You have overcome
Hallelujah

Jesus You have overcome the world
You are ever interceding
As the lost become the found
You can never be defeated
For You wear the Victor's crown
You are Jesus the Messiah
You're the Hope of all the world
By Your grace I live and breathe
To worship You

Hallelujah
You have overcome
You have overcome
Hallelujah
Jesus You have overcome the world
Every high thing must come down
Every stronghold shall be broken
You wear the Victor's crown
You have overcome
You have overcome
At the cross the work was finished
You were buried in the ground
But the grave could not contain You
For You wear the Victor's crown

Hallelujah
You have overcome
You have overcome
Hallelujah
Jesus You have overcome the world
Every high thing must come down
Every stronghold shall be broken
You wear the Victor's crown
You have overcome
You have overcome

14

DECLARATIONS!

Write the following down on paper and tape these on your bathroom mirrors, above your kitchen sink, and on the doors to your home anywhere where you will see it often.

Say this out loud every time you stand in front of it. Say it with gusto! Say it loud!

"I am a child of the Most High God. I have the mind of Christ. Great is my peace. My home is flooded with shalom peace. Angels encamp around my family and me. They protect my family and me and are ministering to me even now. No weapon formed against us will prosper in Jesus' name. The Holy Spirit is my counselor and dearest friend. He will never leave me nor forsake me. I have the keys to the kingdom, whatever I bind on earth is surely bound in Heaven. I bind all powers and works of darkness in or around my home, family or myself that may be present. I decree the Father's will BE DONE in my life, my family's life and in my child's life on earth as it is in Heaven. I have lovely thoughts that produce lovely fruit in my life.

I am filled to overflowing with love for my child. God is working things out for great good in my life. Every day will only get brighter with the Light and Love of Christ Jesus in my heart and life. I have faith in God. He is trustworthy. If He promised it, then I can count on Him."

Our words define the boundaries of blessings in our lives. This day, we will speak bountiful blessings over our families together! We'll do this together!

GOD SPEAKS:

"Let the words of my mouth and the meditation of my heart be acceptable in your sight, O LORD, my rock and my redeemer." (Psalm 19:14 ESV)

"From the fruit of a man's mouth his stomach is satisfied; he is satisfied by the yield of his lips. Death and life are in the power of the tongue, and those who love it will eat its fruits." (Proverbs 18:20-go ESV)

"From the fruit of his mouth a man eats what is good, but the desire of the treacherous is for violence. Whoever guards his mouth preserves his life; he who opens wide his lips comes to ruin."(Proverbs 13:2ESV)

LET'S WORSHIP TOGETHER!

Hallelujah Praise, CeCe Winans

Hallelujah, Hallelujah, Hallelujah, Hallelujah, Hallelujah,
Hallelujah, Hallelujah is the highest praise,
Hallelujah is the highest praise, Hallelujah is the highest praise,
Hallelujah is the highest praise

[Chorus]

Let everything that hath breath, praise the Lord
Come on and sing, be joyful unto the Lord
Let everything that hath breath, praise the Lord
Come on and sing, let everything
Sun and the moon, all stars of light
He commanded and they were created
Oh trumpets sound, throughout the earth
For the Lord is good and greatly to be praised

[Repeat Chorus]

Let the high praise be in your mouth, Bless His holy name forever, ever
Young and the old, all God's children
Let's praise Him, and Him alone

[Repeat Chorus]

[Bridge]

Praise Him for (Praise Him for His mighty acts), Praise Him for
(Praise Him for His goodness), Praise Him for (Praise Him for His
Holy Name), (Praise Him with timbrel and dance)

[Repeat]

Throw up my hands, raise my voice
Move my feet, I will rejoice

[repeat]
Can't help but praise Him

[repeat]
Move, and let me praise Him

[repeat]
So raise your hands, move side to side Give up the praise, let God arise
Can't help but praise Him

15
TRUE CONFESSIONS

I wish I could say that the name of the person involved has been changed to protect their identity, but I cannot. It was me. This is a true story.

I wanted to get as close to God as I could. I did not understand that as a Believer I could not be any closer to him than I already was. In my pursuit, I did some really dumb things. Had I known the scriptures well, I would have known the truth and that truth would have saved me from being a laughing stock to my enemy.

I actually climbed a wobbly ladder onto the roof of my house holding a poster sized message to God. I can't believe I actually did that, but I did. I just wanted to be as close to Him as I possibly could and out of sheer ignorance I thought altitude would do it for me!

The enemy knows who we are, he can see the spirit of God inside of us. He knows what Jesus did for us. He's hoping that we never truly come to the understanding of who we are in Christ Jesus and what that means for our families and our children in need of freedom from defect.

If God were to come down from Heaven and visit you, would that make you more brave? You know where I'm going with this…He has already come down from Heaven and lives inside of you as a Believer. We can stand strong and confident, knowing that every step we take, the Spirit of God takes with us.
We'll march together on this road to freedom for our children, and the Spirit of the Living God will be with us every step of the way.

If you've been feeling desperate for God to come and help you, you can come down off your 'roof' now. God is here. He's with you today. Bank on it!

GOD SPEAKS:

"But he who is joined to the Lord becomes one spirit with him."
(1 Corinthians 6:17 ESV)

"I do not ask for these only, but also for those who will believe in me through their word, that they may all be one, just as you, Father, are in me, and I in you, that they also may be in us, so that the world may believe that you have sent me. The glory that you have given me I have given to them, that they may be one even as we are one, I in them and you in me, that they may become perfectly one, so that the world may know that you sent me and loved them even as you loved me."(John 17:20-23 ESV)

LET'S WORSHIP TOGETHER!

"God in Me", Daniel Doss Band

It's not the melody that brings me to You, It's not even the words that burn in my heart, It's not the wonderful sounds that cause me to sing, It is knowing You and what You've done in me

You are the song of my life, You are the dance in my feet, You are the voice of my heart, You are God in me, You are the bread of my life, You are the life giving drink, You are the everything, You are God in me, yeah

So I will sing my life a song to remain, And whatever I do it's all for Your fame, Because it's your beautiful self that causes me to sing, About knowing You and what You do in me

You are the dance in my feet, You are the voice of my heart, You are God in me,, You are the bread of my life, You are the life giving drink, You are the everything, You are God in me

Yeah, me in You and You in me, I will never stop knowing the joy that You bring And me in You and You in me, I will never stop tasting, tasting Your goodness

16

XXX POISON - BEWARE!

The life of God, that life that is present in every Believer, flows out of our spirits, through our souls (minds, will, emotions) continuing out through our physical bodies and into those around us destroying the works of the devil and restoring order and perfection. Quite specifically the Word of God says in John 7:38," Whoever believes in me, as the scripture hath said, out of his belly shall flow rivers of living water".

If our souls are contaminated, then the flow of life from our spirits could slow to a trickle and possibly even be stopped altogether.

How do we contaminate our souls? Contamination would be anything that would get us out into the "soulish realm". The sin of offense, unrighteous anger, ungodly sorrow or anything that would take our eyes off of the truth and onto a lie would be contaminating our souls.

This is why renewing our minds is vital to successfully ministering healing to our children diagnosed with birth defect. When you are reading about the diagnosis your child has been given, and listening to the reports from doctors, therapists, family, friends, and church members in light of it being a "gift from God" and "incurable", this can consume your attention and damage your faith. When you are opposed by these same people for wanting your child healed completely from the birth defect, then you are, in essence, a salmon swimming upstream. It is challenging to stand in faith for something that looks you in the eyes daily and screams "defect". To survive successfully on a daily basis, you have to be more convinced of what you do not see than what you are seeing. "Now faith is the substance of things not seen the evidence of things hoped for" (Hebrews 11:1).

To make it simple, you have to have more Word of God in you than anybody else's word or thought. If you are going to be distracted, then it should be a Godly distraction. If you are going to be entertained, then it should be something that will not harm your faith. You must be more convinced of the 'truth not seen' than the reason and logic that is seen. This is what pleases God and this is what is necessary to strengthen the spirit and avoid getting into the soulish realm.

I am regularly evaluating my effectiveness as a parent who is consistently ministering healing to my child diagnosed with birth defect. I have known through experience that the resurrection power of God would flow more freely when I was not distracted by anything but walking in the goodness of God and his faithfulness. I have had days that I was on my knees crying with deep sorrow to God because of the visible attack on my daughter. Sometimes the distraction of the disease has derailed my joy and gotten me into the soulish realm and into a place of ineffective prayer. I firmly believe that when given the opportunity, the devil will exacerbate the wounded parent who is operating in the soulish realm. He doesn't want us to know that we truly ARE the solution to the problem. He wants us to think that we couldn't possibly minister healing effectively to our children and get results. When a parent is operating in the soulish realm, they will have little power to overcome the wiles of the devil and minister healing to their child.

Awareness of the enemy's job to get our souls contaminated is paramount in walking our days out in victory. It will take discipline to keep our minds renewed, and help of the Holy Spirit to offset the enemy's attempts to shove us into the soulish realm.

How can we put this truth into action? We will maintain a disciplined lifestyle of spending time with our Father and reading and studying His words to us. We will take care of our physical bodies, so that they operate well. We can command our minds to submit to the truth of the Word of God no matter what we see with our natural eyes. We will be aware of the trickeries of the enemy and make our minds to be distracted with what we choose, not what the enemy chooses.

We have what is necessary to overcome the enemy's attempts to contaminate our souls and render us useless for our Kingdom. We have the spirit of the living God dwelling inside of us, who is our counselor and helper.

You **can** do this. We'll do it together!

GOD SPEAKS:

"We destroy arguments and every lofty opinion raised against the knowledge of God, and take every thought captive to obey Christ".(2 Corinthians 10:5 ESV)

"His divine power has granted to us all things that pertain to life and godliness, through the knowledge of him who called us to his own glory and excellence, by which he has granted to us his precious and very great promises, so that through them you may become partakers of the divine nature, having escaped from the corruption that is in the world because of sinful desire."(2 Peter 1:3-4 ESV)

LET'S WORSHIP TOGETHER!

The Word of God Video,
Seeds Family Worship

The Word of God is living and active, sharper than any two-edged sword,

The Word of God is living and active, sharper than any two-edged sword,

Piercing to the division of soul and spirit, of joints and marrow,

discerning the thoughts and intentions of the heart

(chorus)

I love your Word, I love your Word, oh God, I love your Word,

I love your Word, I love your Word, oh God, I love your Word

The Word of God is living and active sharper than two-edged sword

The Word of God is living and active sharper than any two-edged sword

Piercing to the division of soul and spirit, of joints and marrow

discerning the thoughts and intentions of the heart

(Chorus)

We Love your Word, we love your Word oh God,

We love your Word, We love your Word oh God

17

NEED MORE PATIENCE?

IMPOSSIBLE!

The Bible clearly states that you already possess everything you need for life and Godliness (see 2 Peter 1:3). Your character and nature is kind, loving, gentle, self-controlled, and patient because you are IN Christ Jesus. If you are a **Believer**, then this is the truth.

You are being a hypocrite when you act the opposite of Jesus, not the other way around. As a Child of God, dearly loved, and not without His Help...as a joint heir with Jesus Christ...as the Beloved...having the nature of your Father...Stand up straight! Hold your head up. You are who the Bible says you are. You have what the Bible says you have. Easier said than done?

How do we bridge the gap between what we know is the truth and what the Bible says about us, and actually experiencing it? I've got a personal example that demonstrates the only bridge that connects the knowledge that we have unlimited fruit of the Spirit and the experiencing this in our daily lives.

It was the year 1999 and we lived in St. Louis at the time. I had given birth to our third child, a perfect and healthy baby girl. All three children were still young enough to be in diapers. My emotional state went haywire and I cried every day for a month. I'm sure that my hormones were unbalanced and honestly, three in diapers was uncharted waters for this mother!

I reasoned that there had to be a "happy pill (antidepressant) that the doctor could prescribe. I thought that if I could take a pill, I would stop all the crying and be happy again.

Well, I got to enjoy five days of that "happy pill" (antidepressant) before my pediatrician scolded me and told me to either quit nursing my newborn or get off that pill! I chose to "get off that pill", but the euphoria I experienced from that 'happy pill' would not be forgotten.

Fast forward about twelve months when all of my children were diagnosed with a serious respiratory virus, RSV. (This was years before I knew how to effectively pray regarding sickness & disease.) There was excessive coughing, thick congestion and high fevers. It was 1 o'clock on a Saturday afternoon and I was still in my nightgown. Everyone was sleeping in the house except for our two-year-old son who could not be allowed to be the only person in the house awake and mobile. That would be a recipe for disaster! In my weakened and worn out state, I postured myself on my knees preparing to beg God for kindness and patience towards my child who refused to sleep. My prayer started with "Lord, please give me patience and kindness...then Galatians 5:22 and John 15:5 collided into a Holy Spirit experience I will never forget!

I realized I already had patience and kindness because I was "attached to the vine" and the Bible said that if I was attached to the vine I would produce the fruit of the Spirit! I legitimately possessed patience and kindness without measure!

Then suddenly it happened! This mainstream denominational mama had a supernatural experience! My body was flooded with what felt like the "happy pill". <u>I experienced patience - without measure- when I recognized that I already had it.</u> This was borne out of hiding the Word in my heart day after day.

Though the feelings of that experience wore off, the reality of the fruit of the Spirit and how it is produced in my life never has. (**Feelings are <u>NOT</u> necessary in experiencing what the Bible says is ours**).

The 'how' it works question is cemented in the faith factor. <u>Faith is the bridge that joins truth with experience.</u> You must believe what the Bible says about you before you can walk in it. Remember, feelings do not navigate our limits to things like patience and kindness and self-control. Faith in the Word of God and what He says about us sets our limits and boundaries on our patience, kindness, self-control- on ALL the fruit of the Spirit.

We will stay in faith today, act out what we know to be true about ourselves, no matter how we feel. We'll do it together!

GOD SPEAKS:

"Now faith is the assurance of things hoped for, the conviction of things not seen". (Hebrews 11:1 ESV)

"I am the vine; you are the branches. Whoever abides in me and I in him, he it is that bears much fruit, for apart from me you can do nothing".(John 15:5 ESV)

"But the fruit of the Spirit is love, joy, peace, patience, kindness, goodness, faithfulness, gentleness, self-control; against such things there is no law".(Galatians 5:22-23 ESV)

LET'S WORSHIP TOGETHER!

*What would it look like if you truly stood to your feet right now and purposely worshipped our God and our Savior Jesus Christ with all of your might for six minutes and fifty-five seconds? Let's do it together!

Happy Day, Jesus Culture

The greatest day in history, death is beaten. You have rescued me.

Sing it out, Jesus is alive. The empty cross, the empty grave.

Life eternal, You have won the day. Shout it all, Jesus is alive,

He's alive

Chorus:

Oh happy day, happy day. You washed my sin away.

Oh happy day, happy day I'll never be the same.

Forever I am changed When I stand, in that place.

Free at last, meeting face to face. I am Yours, Jesus You are mine.

Endless joy, perfect peace. Earthly pain finally will cease.

Celebrate Jesus is alive. He's alive

Bridge:

Oh what a glorious day. What a glorious way.

That You have saved me. Oh what a glorious day.

What a glorious name

18

BOOT CAMP FOR YOUR BRAIN!

Are you in a tailspin of negative emotions? Believe me, I understand. I've 'been there and done that'...but I don't do that anymore. It's time to take charge of what you are thinking on!

What has happened is this: the enemy has been successful in gaining access to your thoughts, and you have believed some of his lies. Life is not as bad as you think it is. Remember, as Believers, when the enemy sees you, he also sees the Spirit of God. He is simply working overtime using his strategies of war to distract you from the truth. If he is having success with this in your life, chances are he's not going to try something new. So it's up to you and me to break the cycle of negativity in our lives.

It's time to engage in <u>immediate</u> mental ***"lockdown"!***

We need to control every thought that goes into our brains. This can be a challenge when you are in a state of emergency concerning your emotions and thoughts.

Here is **Boot camp for your brain 101**:

Force your brain to think on what you want it to by creating an environment filled with the truth,

Here are some options[2] of what you could be playing nonstop in your home, car or "as you go":

- Worship Music!

- <u>Divine Healing Training</u>- Curry Blake
  *New Man Series-Curry Blake (JGLM.org)

- Any Sermon by Andy Hayner
  (FullSpeedImpact.com)

- *Any Sermon by Dan Mohler (Youtube)

- * Any sermon by Pete Cabrera, Jr. (Youtube)

And for goodness sake LISTEN to what is being played...don't tune it out. Force yourself to listen. Also, let your prayer buddy and anyone who is standing in faith with you know that you are in a state of emotional emergency. In addition to hearing the truth, you need to take some other actions as well. Here are some lovely additional actions that I strongly suggest. You won't be alone in this, we will do this together!

- Take a walk outside and purposefully use all your senses to experience the fresh outdoors

- Plan a lovely meal

- Clean out a closet

---

[2] The resources that I mention in this section are available on YouTube.

- Read that book you've been wanting to read

- Make a coffee date with a friend and keep it (consider a coffee date with a friend over skype or the phone if you are unable to leave your home)

- Incorporate some type of aerobic exercise in your week...last week I grabbed two cans of refried beans to use as exercise weights! Be creative with your resources to exercise. You're not alone in this. Remember, we're doing this together!

- Choose to believe that life is not as bad as you may have thought. Choose to believe that with God surely the clouds will blow over and the sunshine that's been there all the while will shine bright again!

- Pray for someone in need. You reap what you sow. Sow encouragement in someone today!

- Spend quiet time reading the Word of God. This proves to be genuine fellowship with the Lord!

The battlefield is not so lonely anymore, because we're standing together in faith!

The most fun suggestion I have for you in "Boot Camp for the Brain" is to meet me on the dance floor of this narrow path of faith and worship our King Jesus together! I'll be waiting for you! Many of us parents will be waiting for you.

GOD SPEAKS:

"It is not what goes into the mouth that defiles a person, but what comes out of the mouth; this defiles a person."
(Matthew 15:11-12 ESV)

"Finally, brothers, whatever is true, whatever is honorable, whatever is just, whatever is pure, whatever is lovely, whatever is commendable, if there is any excellence, if there is anything worthy of praise, think about these things. What you have learned and received and heard and seen in me— practice these things, and the God of peace will be with you."
(Philippians 4:8-9 ESV)

LET'S WORSHIP TOGETHER!

Joyful Joyful, Casting Crowns

Joyful, joyful, we adore You, God of glory, Lord of love;
Hearts unfold like flowers before You, Opening to the sun above.

Joyful, joyful, we adore You, God of glory, Lord of love;
Hearts unfold like flowers before You, Opening to the sun above.
Melt the clouds of sin and sadness; Drive the dark of doubt away;
Joyful, joyful, we adore You, Hearts unfold like flowers before You,

Joyful, joyful, we adore You, Joyful, we adore You
All Your works with joy surround You,
Earth and heaven reflect Your rays, Stars and angels sing around You,
Center of unbroken praise;

Melt the clouds of sin and sadness; Drive the dark of doubt away;
Joyful, joyful, we adore You, Hearts unfold like flowers before You,
Joyful, joyful, we adore You, Joyful, we adore You
God our Father, Christ our Brother, All who live in love are thine;
Teach us how to love each other, Lift us to the joy divine.

Oh, God our Father, Christ our Brother, All who live in love are thine;
Teach us how to love each other, Lift us to the joy divine. Oh, God our
Father, Christ our Brother, All who live in love are thine; Teach us how to
love each other,

Lift us to the joy divine. Joyful, joyful, we adore You, Hearts unfold like
flowers before You, Joyful, joyful, we adore You, Hearts unfold like flowers
before You, Oh, God our Father, Christ our Brother, All who live in love
are thine; Teach us how to love each other

19
LET TRUTH DISTRACT YOU!

It is disturbing to realize that I used to believe that disease had great purpose in my life. I spent over 20 years trying to figure out how to be a better person in the face of difficult circumstances brought on by the diseases that affected my life. I was highly motivated to understand what God was trying to teach me. I wanted to move on from the lifestyle we were living which was riddled with the effects of disease and onto an easier path.

When I found out that this is one of the biggest LIES the enemy has used to beguile the church, it was game over! FREEDOM had come into my life because the truth had been found. The truth sets people free, not disease.

Don't be distracted by what the enemy has done this day in your child, choose to be distracted by the **truth**. Thank the Lord for perfection in their appearance. Thank the Lord for perfection in their development. Thank the Lord that ALL the answers to His promises are 'YES'! (see 1 Corinthians 1:20).

We have choices. We get to choose our responses to what we hear and see. Carnal people respond to what they hear, see and feel…but those led by the spirit respond in a way the world will never understand. We respond to the unseen truths about our children and we call it forth in Jesus' name! We can choose to be distracted this day by the truth, not the disease. We'll do it together!

GOD SPEAKS:

"In hope he (Abraham) believed against hope, that he should become the father of many nations, as he had been told, "So shall your offspring be." He did not weaken in faith when he considered his own body, which was as good as dead (since he was about a hundred years old), or when he considered the barrenness of Sarah's womb. No unbelief made him waver concerning the promise of God, but he grew strong in his faith as he gave glory to God, fully convinced that God was able to do what he had promised. That is why his faith was "counted to him as righteousness." (Romans 4:18-22 ESV)

"Now faith is the assurance of things hoped for, the conviction of things not seen. For by it the people of old received their commendation. By faith we understand that the universe was created by the word of God, so that what is seen was not made out of things that are visible." (Hebrews 11:1 ESV)

"Therefore, since we are surrounded by so great a cloud of witnesses, let us also lay aside every weight, and sin which clings so closely, and let us run with endurance the race that is set before us, looking to Jesus, the founder and perfecter of our faith..." (Hebrews 12:1-2 ESV)

LET'S WORSHIP TOGETHER!

<u>The Rock Won't Move</u>, Vertical church

When the ground beneath my feet gives way, And I hear the sound of crashing waves, All my world is washing out to sea, I'm hidden safe in the God who never moves Holding fast to the promise of the truth, That You are holding tighter still to me,

The Rock won't move and His word is strong, The Rock won't move and His love can't be undone, The Rock won't move and His word is strong, The Rock won't move and His love can't be undone

The Rock of our Salvation, My hope is in the promise of Your blood, My support within the raging flood, Even in the tempest, I can sing, I'm hidden safe in the God who never moves, Holding fast to the promise of Your truth, That You are holding tighter still to me

The Rock won't move and His word is strong,

The Rock won't move and His love can't be undone, The Rock won't move and His word is strong, The Rock won't move and His love can't be undone The Rock of our Salvation, Woah, woah, Woah, the Rock of our salvation, On Christ the Solid Rock I stand, All other ground is sinking sand, The Rock won't move, the Rock won't move, When darkness seems to hide His face, I rest on His unchanging grace

The Rock won't move, the Rock won't move, The Rock won't move and His word is strong, The Rock won't move and His love can't be undone, The Rock won't move and His word is strong, The Rock won't move and His love can't be undone

20

ARE WE THERE YET?

Ever feel that way about your child's manifested healing?
Why isn't it 'done' yet? Maybe you're like me and you've
witnessed amazing and miraculous changes both physically
and mentally, but the traces of the diagnosis are still evident
to you and even strangers take notice.

We've decided to take God at His Word, right? We made a
choice to believe that not only is it possible that our children
could be healed, but we are convinced that Jesus has already
paid the price for perfection in full and we aren't backing
down in our faith for the complete manifestation of the
promise. We're on the same page, right?

But maybe you're asking 'why didn't this happen yesterday'?
Nobody likes to be in a car with a child who is constantly
asking, "are we there yet?" It's an irritant.

A friend of mine, Marina, ministering healing to her son
diagnosed with down syndrome, told me that we should
consider the days we are ministering healing to our children
as a 'ride on an airplane to a vacation in Hawaii'. She suggests
that we put on the headphones and crank up the worship
music!

This perspective gets rid of that 'are we there yet mindset'
and makes the journey much sweeter!

Our days of ministering healing to our children are not in vain and they won't last forever. Let's make this road to freedom for our children a sweet adventure of faith. It will take a determined mindset to accomplish this. We won't shelve our expectations for constant changes toward perfection. We will Keep our eyes and expectations focused straight ahead knowing that our Good and Faithful God will not go back on His Word, which is our firm foundation!

Turn the volume up when it's time to worship! Let's do it together!

GOD SPEAKS:

"Finally, be strong in the Lord and in the strength of his might. Put on the whole armor of God, that you may be able to stand against the schemes of the devil. For we do not wrestle against flesh and blood, but against the rulers, against the authorities, against the cosmic powers over this present darkness, against the spiritual forces of evil in the heavenly places. Therefore take up the whole armor of God, that you may be able to withstand in the evil day, and having done all, to stand firm. Stand therefore, having fastened on the belt of truth, and having put on the breastplate of righteousness, and, as shoes for your feet, having put on the readiness given by the gospel of peace. In all circumstances take up the shield of faith, with which you can extinguish all the flaming darts of the evil one; and take the helmet of salvation, and the sword of the Spirit, which is the word of God, praying at all times in the Spirit, with all prayer and supplication."
(Ephesians 6:10-18 ESV).

LET'S WORSHIP TOGETHER!

Jesus Firm Foundation

Mike Donehey, Steven Curtis Chapman, Mark Hall & Mandisa

How firm a foundation, you saints of the Lord, Is laid for your faith in his excellent word, What more can he say than to you he has said, To you who for refuge to Jesus have fled

Fear not, he is with us, oh be not dismayed, For he is our god, our sustainer and strength, He'll be our defender and cause us to stand, Upheld by his merciful, almighty hand

How firm, our foundation, How sure, our salvation, And we will not be shaken
Jesus, firm foundation

The soul that is trusting in Jesus as Lord, Will press on enduring the darkest of storm, And though even hell should endeavor to shake, He'll never, no never, no no never forsake, He'll never, no never, no no never forsake

Age to age he stands, Faithful to the end, All may fade away, But he will remain
He will remain!

21

NO LONGER

A SLAVE TO FEAR

When we are fearful, we are not being faithful. When we get distracted by comments and reactions from man that lead us into fear, we must take time to reestablish our position of faith.

I'm not saying that we need to be completely comfortable in the face of man's opposition to our belief that God wills our children free from birth defect. How could we? We know the truth. We understand what Jesus has purchased for our children in spite of our culture taking a strong stand that is opposite of our faith for our children's healings.

I have had threats and hate mail concerning my desire for my child to be free from birth defect. Maybe you have as well. It's not comfortable.

So how do we walk this out in faith? How do we go to the park, the movies and even church without caving into fear? Hopefully our children's manifested healings are today, but if it lingers, we need a plan of action to squelch this demonic attack against our joy, peace and faith.

Can we be free from fear? The Bible says we can! "I sought the LORD, and he answered me and delivered me from all my fears". (Psalm 34:4 ESV)

The Lord is our deliverer.

We can learn from Daniel how to remain in faith as our children are walking out their healing.

The Old Testament prophet Daniel was kidnapped and taken hundreds of miles from home. He not only could not speak the language of the new country he was a slave to, but the customs, sights and smells were foreign as well. He was truly a foreigner in the land, but he did not bow his knee to the foreign gods in Babylon. He remained true to God despite his foreign surroundings.

Daniel lived in the midst of a government that completely opposed his beliefs, yet he remained calm in the midst of opposition. What was his secret? I believe Daniel's secret to peaceful living in the midst of opposition was found in his relationship with God. Daniel's relationship with God was uncompromised by schedule or man's pressures. He kept his relationship with God a priority, spending time in prayer three times a day with his maker.

Now, let's get back to the playground and the places that make you uncomfortable when you think about visiting with your child. How do we bring peace to those moments in our day?

Here's my P.O.A. (plan of action):

Spend regular appointed time with the Father in solitude and prayer.

When we go to these arenas that have in the past brought about fear, let's be aware that God is with us! Picture the Father standing with you and your child at the park or grocery store. If fear tries to come upon you, resist it by remembering that God is there with you (his spirit is literally inside of you!). Acknowledge God's presence in your mind the moment you sense fear because, 'there is no fear in love, but perfect love casts out fear."(1 John 4:18 ESV)

GOD SPEAKS:

"Let the words of my mouth and the meditation of my heart be acceptable in your sight, O LORD, my rock and my redeemer." (Psalm 19:14 ESV)

"From the fruit of a man's mouth his stomach is satisfied; he is satisfied by the yield of his lips. Death and life are in the power of the tongue, and those who love it will eat its fruits." (Proverbs 18:20-21 ESV)

'From the fruit of his mouth a man eats what is good, but the desire of the treacherous is for violence. Whoever guards his mouth preserves his life; he who opens wide his lips comes to ruin.'(Proverbs 13:2-3 ESV)

LET'S WORSHIP TOGETHER!
No Longer Slaves,
Bethel Music

You unravel me, with a melody You surround me with a song
Of deliverance, from my enemies Till all my fears are gone

I'm no longer a slave to fear I am a child of God
I'm no longer a slave to fear I am a child of God

From my mothers womb You have chosen me
Love has called my name I've been born again, into your family
Your blood flows through my veins

I'm no longer a slave to fear I am a child of God
I'm no longer a slave to fear I am a child of God

I am surrounded By the arms of the father I am surrounded
By songs of deliverance We've been liberated From our bondage
Were the sons and the daughters

Let us sing our freedom You split the sea
So I could walk right through it All my fears were drowned in perfect
love You rescued me So I could stand and sing I am child of God

22

IMPORTANT THINGS NOT TO FORGET!

Reminder:

God is with you and for you. You are an overcomer. Remember, to be an overcomer, there must be something to overcome! It is inside of you to persevere. You have what it takes to make it to the finish line. You can do this!

You can do ALL things through Christ who will continue to give you the strength you need. (see Philippians 4:13) We'll do it together!

Be practical:

Get reasonable amounts of sleep. You need to take care of yourself.

Treat yourself to a special cup of tea or a good cup of coffee.

Spend time reading the Word of God in a quiet place in your day. You may be thinking, 'there is no quiet place in my day'! I don't believe that. Now, I do not know what you do from the moment your child starts their day. You may be feeding them through a tube and changing their adult diapers. That takes a lot of physical and mental endurance, no doubt.

I have done some hard things in the last many years, but when I want it, I have always been able to find a quiet time to read the Word and spend time with my Father. It is always planned out and usually costs something. That 'something' is usually sleep! The Holy Spirit will help you find this precious time if you ask him.

This is our primary relationship and should be the most important focus in our lives. As challenging as it can be, let us be purposeful in carving out time to spend with our Father in His Word.

In doing this, you are spending special time with the Lover of your soul and Creator of the Universe!! Most certainly, we will do this together!

GOD SPEAKS:

"O God, you are my God; earnestly I seek you; my soul thirsts for you; my flesh faints for you, as in a dry and weary land where there is no water. So I have looked upon you in the sanctuary, beholding your power and glory. Because your steadfast love is better than life, my lips will praise you. So I will bless you as long as I live; in your name I will lift up my hands. My soul will be satisfied as with fat and rich food, and my mouth will praise you with joyful lips, when I remember you upon my bed, and meditate on you in the watches of the night; for you have been my help, and in the shadow of your wings I will sing for joy. My soul clings to you; your right hand upholds me.

But those who seek to destroy my life (my child's life) shall go down into the depths of the earth; they shall be given over to the power of the sword; they shall be a portion for jackals. But the king shall rejoice in God; all who swear by him shall exult, for the mouths of liars will be stopped." (Psalm 63:1-11 ESV)

"Draw near to God, and he will draw near to you. Cleanse your hands, you sinners, and purify your hearts, you double-minded." (James 4:8 ESV)

LET'S WORSHIP TOGETHER!

Remembrance , Matt Maher

Oh, how could it be, That my God would welcome me into this mystery,
Say take this bread, take this wine, Now the simple made divine for any to
receive

By Your mercy, we come to Your table, By Your grace, You are making us
faithful Lord, we remember You, And remembrance leads us to worship,
And as we worship You, Our worship leads to communion,
We respond to Your invitation, we remember You

See His body, His blood, Know that He has overcome every trial we will
face, None too lost to be saved, None too broken or ashamed, all are
welcome in this place

By Your mercy, we come to Your table, By Your grace, You are making us
faithful, Lord, we remember You, And remembrance leads us to worship,
And as we worship You, Our worship leads to communion, We respond to
Your invitation, we remember You

Dying You destroyed our death, Rising You restored our life, Lord Jesus,
come in glory Lord Jesus, come in glory, Lord Jesus, come in glory, Lord
Jesus, come in glory

Lord, we remember You, And remembrance leads us to worship, And as
we worship You, Our worship leads to communion, We respond to Your
invitation, We respond to Your invitation, we remember You

23
EXPECTANT FAITH

It is NOT God's will for any of our children to have a trace of defect..."on earth as it is in Heaven"...clearly this is God's will. Together we have made the choice to take God at his word, believe his promises and expect them to manifest in our children!

And that is what this movement of God is about...bringing God's will to earth, enforcing His will be done, with even a mustard sized seed of faith...expecting what Jesus did at the whipping post to be accomplished in our children NOW ...not when they die. Healing isn't accomplished when they die. A buried body with disease is a body that did not receive healing.

Be of good courage. Healing is not a random act of Jesus. He poured out his blood and bares the scars in his flesh for our children's healings. It is the Word of God. It is coming to pass. "Why isn't it overnight", you may be asking. Let's expect that! What Jesus did cannot be altered. He did it. He carried the disease of down syndrome and autism and all manner of birth defect so our children would not have to.

Expect the symptoms of defect to go in the name of Jesus. Expect the Holy Spirit to flow out of your spirit into your child's body to bring divine order. Do not quit expecting our Good Creator Father's words to come to pass. Do not retreat and take your faith back!

It is a matter of time for the fruition of the promises to manifest. Something is going to change during this time, either you will change your faith or our children's genetic defect will change. We are not letting up on our faith. It's the Word of God. His Word is our final authority. It's a 'no brainer'; we choose to stand firm and believe.

Expect change. Expect what you are decreeing. Expect those chromosomes to be perfect. Expect breathing to be normal and healthy. Expect speech. Expect muscles to strengthen. Expect bones to grow. Expect the nose to grow. Expect beauty. Expect defective fat to vanish. Expect perfected brains. Expect God's word not to return void. By Jesus' stripes your child is healed and ALL things contrary to this must GO in the name of Jesus. We agree on this!

Onward March! We'll do this together!

GOD SPEAKS

God is not man, that he should lie, or a son of man, that he should change his mind. Has he said, and will he not do it? Or has he spoken, and will he not fulfill it?

(Numbers 23:19 ESV)

"Blessed is the man who trusts in the LORD, whose trust is the LORD. He is like a tree planted by water, that sends out its roots by the stream, and does not fear when heat comes, for its leaves remain green, and is not anxious in the year of drought, for it does not cease to bear fruit." (Jeremiah 17:7-8 ESV)

LET'S WORSHIP TOGETHER!

Nothing is Impossible, Planet shakers

Through You I can do anything, I can do all things,
'Cause it's You who gives me strength, Nothing is impossible,
Through You blind eyes are open, Strongholds are broken,

I am living by faith, Nothing is impossible I'm not gonna live by what I
see, I'm not gonna live by what I feel, Deep down I know that You're
here with me, And I know that You can do anything

Through You I can do anything, I can do all things, 'Cause it's You
who gives me strength,

Nothing is impossible, Through You blind eyes are open, Strongholds
are broken, I am living by faith,

Nothing is impossible, Nothing is impossible
I'm not gonna live by what I see,

I'm not gonna live by what I feel, Deep down I know that You're here with
me, And I know that You can do anything I believe, I believe, I believe, I
believe in you, I believe, I believe, I believe, I believe in you, I believe, I
believe, I believe, I believe in you, I believe, I believe, I believe, I believe in
you

24

THE REALITY OF CHILDREN OF GOD SPEAKING TO THE MOUNTAINS!

Jesus talked to a fig tree and told us to speak to mountains. Why then would it seem odd to speak to a chromosome, a bone, a brain or a toe?

At the beginning of creation, we were given dominion on this planet over every living thing. When you have dominion over something, you have the authority to tell it what to do and it must obey. In the Strong's Concordance, this word 'dominion' is a Greek word that means exactly what it says. It means to have dominion, prevail against, reign, and rule over.

When you factor in the whipping post and what the Bible says Jesus did for us there, coupled with our position of dominion given to us by God on this planet way back in Genesis, we should be able to confidently approach any birth defect symptom or diagnosis, and expect it to go.

Clearly the Lord has told us that our enemy immediately comes to steal the Promises when we hear what they are. That nasty old devil, the enemy of God and His children, has been busy trying to make us think we are powerless beggars orphaned by a god who delights in giving babies' diseases that keep them from abundant life. We are in fact the ones who hold all the cards. My friend, Andy Hayner, puts it like this: "We hold the biggest gun in the battle"!

I am getting so excited just writing down the truths of what we have as Children of God, joint heirs with Jesus, and recipients of the finished work that Jesus did at the whipping post! Honestly, if the church ever gets understanding in this, the entire planet will be flooded with the manifested children of God who will be eradicating all manners of sicknesses and diseases including birth defects! It's coming, it's just a matter of time.

We minister healing to our children with Jesus as our model. He effectively healed people in various ways, let's take our cues from him. He laid hands on the sick. He commanded the disease to go. He told the bodies what to do. He did it from a distance and he did it in person. You can pray for your child effectively anywhere at any time with words or just the laying on of hands. We are joint heirs with Jesus, having the same spirit that raised him from the dead inside of us and the rights to using his name for the freedom of our children and anyone in need of healing. Game on! We'll do it together!

GOD SPEAKS:

"Truly, I say to you, among those born of women there has arisen no one greater than John the Baptist. Yet the one who is least in the kingdom of heaven is greater than he."
(Matthew 11:11 ESV)

"As they passed by in the morning, they saw the fig tree withered away to its roots. And Peter remembered and said to him, "Rabbi, look! The fig tree that you cursed has withered." And Jesus answered them, "Have faith in God. Truly, I say to you, whoever says to this mountain, 'Be taken up and thrown into the sea,' and does not doubt in his heart, but believes that what he says will come to pass, it will be done for him. Therefore I tell you, whatever you ask in prayer, believe that you have received it, and it will be yours. And whenever you stand praying, forgive, if you have anything against anyone, so that your Father also who is in heaven may forgive you your trespasses." (Mark 11:20-25)

LET'S WORSHIP TOGETHER!

You Are Here (The Same Power), Hillsong

Same power that conquered the grave,
Lives in me, lives in me,
Your love that rescued the earth,
Lives in me, lives in me
Same power that conquered the grave,
Lives in me, lives in me,
Your love that rescued the earth,
Lives in me, lives in me

25

'FOLLOW THE FAITH

OF THE FAITHFUL'

The following is taken from a message, "Follow the Faith of the Faithful" by Curry Blake originally spoken 12/29/13 with my additions *in* parenthesis

"God is faithful. His word is true. Cut things off out of your life because you can't afford to listen to some people... There are friendships you may have to cut away...I don't care what you are going thru, or what your situation is; every person in this room can absolutely change their mind. How your mind changes: everything you listen to is making a neuro pathway into your mind and it will cause you to think along certain lines.

You can get to a place where you listen to something so much...if you keep listening to people tell you who you are *(what is lacking/diagnosed in your child)*, you'll start believing it, you'll start acting like it is true and it will get engraved in you and you will become that *(you will start expecting that in your child)*.

It is up to you to decide to believe the word of God, and realize what the Word of God says about you *(your child)* and to start to live accordingly and to start cutting off the voices in your life that says contrary to what the Word of God says *(about your child)*. That is a discipline, it's not easy, it's not fun. It'll cost you relationships. It'll cost you friendships. But you have to decide: do you want to be a friend of people or a friend of God. It's just that simple. Usually the people you see that have great faith are people that don't usually have great faith but have great courage and enough courage to cut things out of their lives which includes people that will take them down the wrong path *(which is anything contrary to believing the promises of God for your child)*. You just have to decide where does God want you to go and then surround yourself with people that will help you get there. or at least not hinder you from getting there. Amen."

We'll do it together. The God of angel armies will be with us every step of the way!

GOD SPEAKS:

And Jesus said to him, "... All things are possible for one

who believes." (Mark 9:23 ESV)

"I can do all things through him who strengthens me."
(Philippians 4:13 ESV)

LET'S WORSHIP TOGETHER

Healer, Kari Jobe.

Sung by Tara Ashworth

You hold my every moment, You calm my raging seas,
You walk with me through fire, And heal all my disease,
I trust in You, I trust in You I believe You're my healer, I believe You
are all I need, I believe And I believe You're my portion. I believe
You're more than enough for me. Jesus You're all I need

You hold my every moment. You calm my raging seas. You walk with
me through fire. And heal all my disease. I trust in You, Lord I trust in
You

I believe You're my healer. I believe You are all I need.

Oh, I believe. I believe You're my portion. I believe You're more than
enough for me. Jesus You're all I need Nothing is impossible for You.
Nothing is impossible. Nothing is impossible for You. You hold my
world in Your hands

26

TODAY WE STAND IN FAITH!

Today we stand in faith. We don't need to be concerned about tomorrow or yesterday. Today, we trust our Great God and good Father. His word says our children are already healed.(1 Peter 2:24) We command their bodies to line up with His Words and His Will!

We thank you Holy Spirit for your constant presence and power within us. We submit our minds, our emotions and our will to you. Lead us on in the victory that is ours this day!

All devils and works of devils, we use the keys of the kingdom that Jesus gave us. We bind you. We bind your works.

You are subject to us, Luke 10:19 says this is so. We cancel your lies and plans against us.

Life abundantly is ours this day.

The Father's joy is ours this day.

Shalom peace resides on our heads and our homes this day.

We command our children's bodies to manifest the finished work of our healer, Jesus!

Brains, bodies, toe nails, bones, faces, development, you will line up with the Word of the Creator of the Universe and be perfect.

There is no other option.

Period!

So be it!

Rejoice!

We are not alone, we're doing this together!

GOD SPEAKS:

"...you have received the Spirit of adoption as sons, by whom we cry, "Abba! Father!" The Spirit himself bears witness with our spirit that we are children of God, and if children, then heirs—heirs of God and fellow heirs with Christ...(Romans 8:15-17 ESV)

"He who dwells in the shelter of the Most High
will abide in the shadow of the Almighty.
I will say to the LORD, "My refuge and my fortress,
my God, in whom I trust.
For he will deliver you from the snare of the fowler
and from the deadly pestilence.
He will cover you with his pinions,
and under his wings you will find refuge;
his faithfulness is a shield and buckler.
You will not fear the terror of the night,
nor the arrow that flies by day,
nor the pestilence that stalks in darkness,
nor the destruction that wastes at noonday.
A thousand may fall at your side,
ten thousand at your right hand,
but it will not come near you.
You will only look with your eyes
and see the recompense of the wicked.
Because you have made the LORD your dwelling place—
the Most High, who is my refuge—
no evil shall be allowed to befall you,
no plague come near your tent.
For he will command his angels concerning you to
Guard you in all your ways.
On their hands they will bear you up,
lest you strike your foot against a stone.

You will tread on the lion and the adder;
the young lion and the serpent you will trample underfoot.
"Because he holds fast to me in love, I will deliver him;
I will protect him, because he knows my name.
When he calls to me, I will answer him;
I will be with him in trouble;
I will rescue him and honor him.
With long life I will satisfy him
and show him my salvation." (Psalm 91 ESV)

LET'S WORSHIP TOGETHER!

No Weapon,

Fred Hammond

No weapon formed against me shall prosper, it won't work. No weapon formed against me shall prosper, it won't work. Say no weapon formed against me shall prosper, it won't work. Say no weapon formed against me shall prosper, it won't work

God will do what He said He would do. He will stand by His word. And He will come through. God will do what He said He would do. He will stand by His word. And He will come through.

No weapon formed against me shall prosper, it won't work. No weapon formed against me shall prosper, it won't work God will do what He said He would do. He's not a man that He should lie (Stand by his word).

He will come through. Say God will do what He said He would do. He will stand by His word. He will come through.

Oh I won't be afraid of the arrows by day. From the hand of the enemy. I can stand my ground with the Lord on my side. For the snares they have set will not succeed. No weapon formed against me (shall prosper, it won't work) it won't work. No weapon formed against me (shall prosper) shall prosper, it won't work.

For I know that he'll do (say he'll do it) what he said he's gonna do (say he'll do it). He will stand by his word (stand by his word). He will come through, yeah. God, will do what he said he's gonna do. Stand by his word (stand by his word)

27
"IT'S NOT WORKING!"

Tell me you did NOT just have that thought. Now look me in the eyes and tell me you did not SAY those words out loud, did you? If you did, then get thee behind me, satan. Our Father is not a man that He should lie. (Numbers 32:19) What do you think those Israelites were thinking when they saw that Red Sea before them and their venomous enemy behind them? Do you think they enjoyed that position? You don't have to enjoy the position you are in to be in faith. You have to trust our Creator Father and expect the truth to prevail in your child. It doesn't have to feel good to be faith.

Our experiences are not our doctrine. The Bible is what we believe. It is our standard for living, including what we believe about healing.

Shake off all doubt and unbelief and discouragement and do the 'Avalanche' dance with me today!

GOD SPEAKS:

"Forever, O Lord, your word is firmly fixed in the heavens. Your faithfulness endures to all generations; you have established the earth, and it stands fast. By your appointment they stand this day, for all things are your servants. If your law had not been my delight, I would have perished in my affliction. I will never forget your precepts, for by them you have given me life."(Psalm 119:89-93 ESV)

"Blessed be the Lord! For he has heard the voice of my pleas for mercy. The Lord is my strength and my shield; in him my heart trusts, and I am helped; my heart exults, and with my song I give thanks to him. The Lord is the strength of his people; he is the saving refuge of his anointed." (Psalm 26:6-8 ESV)

"God is not man, that he should lie or a son of man, that he should change his mind. Has he said, and will he not do it? Or has he spoken, and will he not fulfill it?" (Numbers 23:19 ESV)

LET'S WORSHIP TOGETHER!

Hosanna, Kirk Franklin

The angels bow down at the thought of You. The darkness gives way to the light for You. The price that you paid gives us life brand new.

Hosanna, forever we worship You. Hosanna, forever we worship You. Hosanna, forever we worship You. For you are the joy that my soul longs for. The lamb that was slain for my sins and the One I adore.

King of kings, Ruler of everything. Hosanna, forever we worship You. Hosanna, forever we worship You. Hosanna, forever we worship You. For Your patience and kindness. And favor and mercy and honor and glory.

Because You are worthy. We can't live without You. We can't breathe without You. We can't sing without You

Hosanna, Hosanna. No greater love in this world but You. No one can compare to the things You do. Wherever You go, I will follow You. Hosanna, forever we worship You. Hosanna, forever we worship You.

Someday, every tongue shall confess Your name. This house made of clay soon shall pass away. Whatever the test You will bring us through

Hosanna, forever we worship You.

28

THIS TOO SHALL PASS!

I wrote that on my 6th grade math book. I failed one quarter of that year's math class. It was awful. I wasn't gaining enough understanding to pass and I felt defeated before the day began. Do you ever feel that way?

The conflict of believing the promises of God for my daughter while, at times, watching her healing creep as slow as a snail coupled with having my neighbors, oldest friends and much of my family not stand with me has been the biggest obstacle I have ever faced.

A friend of mine recently asked me, "Are you demanding 'her' body to conform to your orders?" She had no idea how encouraging her question was to me. It showed that she not only knew the truth, but cared about my situation with my daughter enough to hold me accountable to be aggressive in my faith. I know that the continual speaking of the Word of God over our children, without family, friends and the church rallying with us in unison can be tiring. The truth is the truth and we expect it to come forth from our children in the name of Jesus! Bodies: conform to the will of God on earth as it is in Heaven!

Certainly you are not alone in this battle. Our great and good Father has seen to that! We are doing this together. Praise the Lord! Be it unto us according to our faith!

GOD SPEAKS:

"Again I say to you, if two of you agree on earth about
anything they ask, it will be done for them by my Father in
heaven." (Matthew 18:19 ESV)

"And as Jesus passed on from there, two blind men followed
him, crying aloud, "Have mercy on us, Son of David." When
he entered the house, the blind men came to him, and Jesus
said to them, "Do you believe that I am able to do this?"
They said to him, "Yes, Lord." Then he touched their eyes,
saying, "According to your faith be it done to you." And their
eyes were opened." (Matthew 9:27-30 ESV)

This would be a wonderful time to take your child's diagnosis report and place it on the kitchen floor and do the 'Avalanche'!

The 'Avalanche ' is a little dance we do when we just need to 'shout out' to Jesus and deliberately and joyfully thank him for what he has done for our children!

Let's do this together!

LET'S WORSHIP TOGETHER
"All Things New", Elevation Worship.
Sung by Tara Ashworth

Peace be still, You are near. There's nowhere we can go
That You won't shine redemption's light Our guilt withdrawn
As You rise, we come alive

The grave has lost, the old is gone And You're making all things new
You are making all things new You are making all things new
And we are free

Hope is found, You are here Our hearts forever sealed By this love that
came for us Now we are Yours As You rise, we come alive

And You're making all things new You are making all things new You
are making all things new And we are free And You're making all
things new You are making all things new God you're making all things
new

And we are free Your love never ending Your grace never failing Redemption is calling us home Your love never ending Your grace never failing Redemption is calling us home

And You're making all things new You are making all things new You are making all things new And we are free And You're making all things new You are making all things new You are making all things new

And we are free And You're making all things new You are making all things new You are making all things new And we are free

29

BATTLE WEARY?

I'VE GOT THE REMEDY!

So you think you are battle weary, do you? Then I believe you're thinking way too much about yourself and way too much about the work of the enemy. A good dose of 'Divine Perspective' is what you need!

What is this Divine Perspective I'm prescribing? It's the "Word of God+Laughter+Cup of Tea+Dancing=Divine Perspective". Take one heaping dose every day!

"Count it all joy, my brothers, when you meet trials of various kinds, for you know that the testing of your faith produces steadfastness. And let steadfastness have its full effect, that you may be perfect and complete, lacking in nothing." (James 1:2-4 ESV)

So you see, our faith is being tested. Our faith is what is at stake. Look, God's got this! Our duty to our Lord and Savior is to keep our eyes on the truth as we are ministering healing to our children. There IS joy to be found even on **this** battlefield.

We stay thankful for what God <u>has</u> done for our kids. We celebrate every small victory on the way to the finish line of complete perfection for our children! And we'll do it together!

Let's do the "Avalanche" together and take a big dose of Divine Perspective together!

GOD SPEAKS:

"Therefore, since we are surrounded by so great a cloud of witnesses, let us also lay aside every weight, and sin which clings so closely, and let us run with endurance the race that is set before us, looking to Jesus, the founder and perfecter of our faith, who for the joy that was set before him endured the cross, despising the shame, and is seated at the right hand of the throne of God." (Hebrews 12:1,2 ESV)

LET'S WORSHIP TOGETHER!

"Victor's Crown", Darlene Zschech.

Sung by Tara Ashworth

You are always fighting for us Heaven's angels all around
My delight is found in knowing That You wear the Victor's crown
You're my help and my defender You're my Saviour and my friend
By Your grace I live and breathe To worship You
At the mention of Your greatness In Your Name I will bow down
In Your presence fear is silent For You wear the Victor's crown
Let Your glory fill this temple Let Your power overflow
By Your grace I live and breathe To worship You Hallelujah
You have overcome You have overcome Hallelujah
Jesus You have overcome the world
You are ever interceding As the lost become the found
You can never be defeated For You wear the Victor's crown
You are Jesus the Messiah You're the Hope of all the world
By Your grace I live and breathe To worship You Hallelujah
You have overcome You have overcome Hallelujah
Jesus You have overcome the world Every high thing must come down
Every stronghold shall be broken You wear the Victor's crown
You have overcome You have overcome At the cross the work was finished
You were buried in the ground But the grave could not contain You
For You wear the Victor's crown
Hallelujah You have overcome You have overcome Hallelujah
Jesus You have overcome the world
Every high thing must come down Every stronghold shall be broken
You wear the Victor's crown You have overcome You have overcome

30
MY PROMISE IS OVERDUE!

You prayed fervently yesterday. You prayed in faith and fervently the day before.

In fact, you've been standing in faith with fervency for way too long. What should you do? You know there isn't anything to add to what you are doing to make it more effective. You can get a sore throat to go. You can get pain off of strangers, and you can even move an ant hill! What is going on?

You have done everything right, and when you felt you might not be doing it right, you got others to minister healing to your child. Not much has changed in your child and you are becoming tired of it all. You cannot embrace the diagnosis, because you know that would conflict with the very core of who you are and what you believe.

What do you do now? YOU STAY THE COURSE! Do not waver. Do not look to the left or to the right. Stay the course.

What do you do when you are distracted by what you see, so much so, that you are unable to rally yourself to pray with fervent faith? How do we put our crumbling hearts in a position of power and authority in order to get this miracle to manifest? Here is my exhortation to you.

Keep your eyes on your target!

These are some excerpts from Joshua 8.

Joshua kept his spear pointed at the walled city of the enemy and the Lord defeated his foe. (Joshua 8:18 ESV) He was told to do this by his God, our God.

The Lord said to Joshua, "Take all the soldiers with you and go on up to Ai. Don't be afraid or discouraged. I will give you victory over the king of Ai; his people, city, and land will be yours." (Joshua 8:1)

The battle was, without question, won by the Lord himself, but Joshua and his army had positions in the battle. They had to *do* something. They had to stand in their positions and were commanded not to be afraid or discouraged. Their victory was promised to them, but they had to remain *in* the battle with direct orders to face their enemy and hold fast to their faith that their God would win the battle for them.

You weren't created to be a robot; you were given a will. It is a matter of choice to resist fear and discouragement, no matter what it feels like. We make our choice this day to resist all feelings of discouragement and fear and take our position in this battle.

Lord, we make a choice today to trust you. We stand together, united on your Word and your promises for our children. Your will BE DONE on earth as it is in Heaven in our children. So be it.

We'll do it together!

GOD SPEAKS:

"Praise the LORD! For it is good to sing praises to our God; for it is pleasant, and a song of praise is fitting. The LORD builds up Jerusalem; he gathers the outcasts of Israel. He heals the brokenhearted and binds up their wounds. He determines the number of the stars; he gives to all of them their names.

Great is our Lord, and abundant in power; his understanding is beyond measure. The LORD lifts up the humble; he casts the wicked to the ground. Sing to the LORD with thanksgiving, make melody to our God on the lyre! He covers the heavens with clouds; he prepares rain for the earth; he makes grass grow on the hills. He gives to the beasts their food, and to the young ravens that cry. His delight is not in the strength of the horse, nor his pleasure in the legs of a man,

but the LORD takes pleasure in those who fear him, in those who hope in his steadfast love. Praise the LORD, O Jerusalem! Praise your God, O Zion! For he strengthens the bars of your gates; he blesses your children within you. He makes peace in your borders; he fills you with the finest of the wheat. He sends out his command to the earth; his word runs swiftly. He gives snow like wool; he scatters frost like ashes. He hurls down his crystals of ice like crumbs; who can stand before his cold?

He sends out his word, and melts them; he makes his wind blow and the waters flow. He declares his word to Jacob, his statutes and rules to Israel. He has not dealt thus with any other nation; they do not know his rules. Praise the LORD!"
(Psalm 147:1-20 ESV)

LET'S WORSHIP TOGETHER!

For the Lamb, Elevation Worship

On a shameful day He died, In the sorrow of defeat, But forgiveness was His cry, As His blood ran down for me How the Father's heart was torn, As His only son was slain, But the earth would soon rejoice, From the place where hope was lain For the Lamb has overcome,

Everlasting love has won, In eternal praise we will lift Him up, For the Lamb has overcome the world By His spirit we are raised, To the fullness of new life, In a moment we'll be changed,

And forever glorified For the Lamb has overcome, Everlasting love has won, In eternal praise we will lift Him up, For the Lamb has overcome the world Most high and lifted up, Be glorified forever, Jesus has overcome, Declare it now together, Most high and lifted up Be glorified forever, Jesus has overcome, Declare it now together Most high and lifted up, Be glorified forever, Jesus has overcome, Declare it now together, Most high and lifted up, Be glorified forever, Jesus has overcome, Declare it now together

For the lamb has overcome, Everlasting love has won, In eternal praise we will lift him up, For the lamb has overcome the world, For the lamb has overcome, Everlasting love has won, In eternal praise we will lift him up, For the lamb has overcome the world, For the lamb has overcome the world, For the lamb has overcome the world

31
"I CAN'T!"

I've washed my children's mouths out with soap for saying those two words.

It's not the truth, those words are simply not the truth.

"I can do all things through him who strengthens me." (Philippians 4:13 ESV) The Word of God is the truth. Maybe we just need to draw a line in the sand today and put the truth on one side and all the facts on the other!

Here is a suggestion for days like this: let's take it to our Father!

He has given us dominion on this planet. This dominion dates back to the Garden of Eden. He never took back that commandment to dominate and rule the earth. This remains. He also gave us everything he gave Jesus! We have inherited his authority and power! He told us to speak to mountains and to decree a thing and it would be established. For goodness sakes, we are new creations, being one in spirit with the Lord himself!

But sometimes we need to just crawl up in our daddy's lap, put our heads on his shoulder and make our requests known to him! He told us to do this as well.

GOD SPEAKS:

"And this is the confidence that we have toward him, that if we ask anything according to his will he hears us. And if we know that he hears us in whatever we ask, we know that we have the requests that we have asked of him."
(1 John 5:14-15 ESV)

"Do not be anxious about anything, but in everything by prayer and supplication with thanksgiving let your requests be made known to God. And the peace of God, which surpasses all understanding, will guard your hearts and your minds in Christ Jesus." (Philippians 4:6-7 ESV)

LET'S WORSHIP TOGETHER!

Praises (Be Lifted Up), Josh Baldwin

I sing praises to Your name, Praises to Your name, The name that's so much higher than all names

All honor to Your name, All honor to Your name, The name that's so much, greater than all names

Be lifted up, Be lifted higher, Be lifted up, Be lifted higher
Your name is life, Your name is hope inside me,
Hope inside me, Your name is love, A love that always finds me,
Always finds me

32
UGH!

I COMPLETELY MESSED UP TODAY!

I am not capable to minister the healing power of God to my child. I am not holy enough. What to do on days like this...

We are under, I said UNDER the blood of Jesus Christ. He has made us right with God. We cannot do ANYTHING to change that. We can't DO anything to be righteous, Jesus has done the work. We just stand up out of our mess and walk forward. Rip the rearview mirror off of that moment and walk forward in who you are.

This is called a 'new covenant mindset', when we fall down and then get right back up, and walk as sons and daughters of the Most High God. We don't have to make atonement for our sins. The atonement for our sins has already occurred. Jesus has paid the price necessary for us to be in good standing with God and to bring his kingdom here on earth.

He paid an enormous price for us to carry his power and presence.

The enemy wants us to think that we are not in a position to speak to mountains, but that old devil is a liar. If Jesus said we could speak to mountains then, by golly, get up and go speak to the mountain! The kingdom of God is at hand! Go lay hands on your child and command that mountain to move!

GOD SPEAKS:

"And these signs will accompany those who believe: in my name they will cast out demons; they will speak in new tongues; they will pick up serpents with their hands; and if they drink any deadly poison, it will not hurt them; they will lay their hands on the sick, and they will recover." (Mark 16:17-18 ESV)

"Truly, truly, I say to you, whoever believes in me will also do the works that I do; and greater works than these will he do, because I am going to the Father. Whatever you ask in my name, this I will do, that the Father may be glorified in the Son. If you ask me anything in my name, I will do it."

(John 14:12-14 ESV)

LET'S WORSHIP TOGETHER!

Your Promises, Elevation Worship

Sung by Tara Ashworth

When the weight of the world begins to fall, On the Name of Jesus I will call, For I know that you are sovereign God and Your purpose is unshakable

[Chorus:]

Doesn't matter what I feel, Doesn't matter what I see, My hope will always be, In Your promises to me, Now I'm casting out all fear, for Your love has set me free, My hope will always be, In Your promises to me

As I walk into the days to come, I will not forget what You have done, For you have supplied my every need, and Your presence is enough for me

You will always be more than enough for me, You will always be more than enough for me, Nothing's gonna stop the plans You've made, Nothing's gonna take Your love away, You will always be more than enough for me.

33
GOOGLE OR BIBLE?

During my first twenty years of marriage, I searched the Bible to find out what it said about healing regarding my husband and the myriad of diagnosis given to him. I wore out the pages and binding of a very large Strong's Concordance with the continuous exploration of the original definitions and meanings of healing scriptures. The conclusion was unwavering; God wanted my husband healed and Jesus had paid for it.

After our 5th child was born and diagnosed with down syndrome, the need for the manifested truth of God's will became an urgent and unabandoned quest.

I googled the words 'healed' and 'down syndrome' and got nothing. I mixed words like "Jesus", "healed" and "birth defect" and still came up empty handed. There seemed to be no precedence for genetic healing that I could find. I was searching for man's experience to dictate whether or not the Scriptures were truth, but I didn't realize I was doing this at the time.

I know I'm not the only one who googled those same words. Maybe you did the same.

The results of googling those same words today are different, *however*, those results are based on people having sure faith on the promises of God.

Faith is what our entire belief structure is built upon. Have you seen Heaven? Probably your answer is 'no', but you believe that it exists, right? Have you seen Jesus? Probably your answer is 'no', but you believe that he is real, right? Your answers reflect your faith. You have faith to believe for something that you have not witnessed with your own experience.

We cannot let man's experience, nor our own experience, dictate what we believe. That would be ludicrous. *"The just shall live by faith."* (Romans 1:17)

We don't have a well-worn path of those who have gone before us, BUT we have the Words of the living God.

I know this is not a fun experience, but when we get home (Heaven) it will be too late to take God at his word. We won't need faith when we get to Heaven, but we need it here and now.

Take courage. Have faith. If you could sit and talk with Jesus and see his scars, you would probably go from that encounter with full assurance of the promises of God. If this were to happen, you would not need faith.

You can build your beliefs upon your experience or you can be a person of faith.

You may be the only person in your town who believes that your child's destiny is being restored through bodily healing; however, you are not the only person on this planet believing the same for their child. <u>We are doing this together!</u>

GOD SPEAKS:

"All Scripture is breathed out by God and profitable for teaching, for reproof, for correction, and for training in righteousness, that the man of God may be complete, equipped for every good work." (2 Timothy 3:16-17 ESV)

'...but my righteous one shall live by faith, and if he shrinks back, my soul has no pleasure in him." But we are not of those who shrink back and are destroyed, but of those who have faith and preserve their souls'. (Hebrews 10:38-39 ESV)

"That is why it depends on faith, in order that the promise may rest on grace and be guaranteed to all his offspring—not only to the adherent of the law but also to the one who shares the faith of Abraham, who is the father of us all, as it is written, "I have made you the father of many nations"—in the presence of the God in whom he believed, who gives life to the dead and calls into existence the things that do not exist. In hope he believed against hope, that he should become the father of many nations, as he had been told, "So shall your offspring be." He did not weaken in faith when he considered his own body, which was as good as dead (since he was about a hundred years old), or when he considered the barrenness of Sarah's womb. No unbelief made him waver concerning the promise of God, but he grew strong in his faith as he gave glory to God, fully convinced that God was able to do what he had promised. That is why his faith was "counted to him as righteousness." (Romans 4:16-22 ESV)

LET'S WORSHIP TOGETHER!

He Is Faithful, Jesus Culture
Sung by Tara Ashworth

I have heard a sound coming on the wind, changing hearts and minds healing brokenness, I hear a generation breaking through despair, I hear a generation full of faith declare, and our song it will be, out of the darkness we will rise and sing

He is faithful, He is glorious, He is Jesus, All my hope is in Him, He is freedom, He is healing right now, He is hope and joy and love and peace and life! I have seen a light like the break of dawn, giving blind men sight, letting lame men walk, I see a generation with resurrection life, we are a generation filled with the power of Christ

He has paid the highest price, He has proven His great love for us, We will praise Him with our lives, And proclaim our love for Him.

34
TOTAL WAR

John 10:10 reveals the root and seed cause of our children's need for freedom from birth defect, as we parents know. This basic understanding positions us on a battlefield that has never before in the history of mankind had an assembling of so great a number of readied soldiers. The enemy is being opposed by an impassioned, organized, and faith filled army of mothers and fathers who are not backing down. We have found the truth and we will not stop until this truth has manifested 100% in our children.

What I believe is presently occurring is that we, the parents, have moved into a position of total war.

There is a myriad of distractions from sunrise to sunset for many of us. Many of these distractions have come in the form of mechanical failures of automobiles, internet connections, dish and clothes washing machine failures, marital and family division, wayward children, financial lack, sleep interruptions, energy draining thoughts, job losses, and various illnesses throughout immediate family members. Much of this is a result of the enemy's war strategy to completely stop our victorious and united march of freedom for our children.

Though most of us are juggling the normal priorities of our marital, parental, job and ministry responsibilities, we also have committed a total effort towards our children's freedom. From sunrise to sunset, much of our resources are supplying our resolve to stay in faith to deflect the incoming barrage of missiles from the enemy, deflect the bombs of discouragement and weariness of our Total War efforts.

So why am I writing the obvious positions of Total War that we, the parents, and our enemy are currently in? I am writing about this because we have the 'biggest gun'. We have the truth. If you don't cave into the constant barrage from the enemy's attempts to make you stop fighting this battle of faith, we will win. Not only will our children win, but quite possibly the church will wake from the slumber of silence in our battle and bring the desperately needed support that she possesses to the parents who will be steps behind us on this battlefield.

You are in Total War, and probably nobody that you know understands this position more clearly than the other parents who are in Total War with you. The frills and bling of life have been redefined or put on hold all because of the intense effort to stay in faith. Stay the course! The victory is imminent.

GOD SPEAKS:

"Finally, be strong in the Lord and in the strength of his might. Put on the whole armor of God, that you may be able to stand against the schemes of the devil. For we do not wrestle against flesh and blood, but against the rulers, against the authorities, against the cosmic powers over this present darkness, against the spiritual forces of evil in the heavenly places. Therefore take up the whole armor of God, that you may be able to withstand in the evil day, and having done all, to stand firm. Stand therefore, having fastened on the belt of truth, and having put on the breastplate of righteousness, and, as shoes for your feet, having put on the readiness given by the gospel of peace. In all circumstances take up the shield of faith, with which you can extinguish all the flaming darts of the evil one; and take the helmet of salvation, and the sword of the Spirit, which is the word of God, praying at all times in the Spirit, with all prayer and supplication. To that end keep alert with all perseverance, making supplication for all the saints, and also for me, that words may be given to me in opening my mouth boldly to proclaim the mystery of the gospel, for which I am an ambassador in chains, that I may declare it boldly, as I ought to speak." (Ephesians 6:10-20)

LET'S WORSHIP TOGETHER!

My Jesus I love Thee (Your Holy Name),
Building 429

My Jesus, I love Thee, I know Thou art mine. For Thee all the follies of sin I resign. My gracious Redeemer, my Savior art Thou. If ever I loved Thee, my Jesus 'tis now

Worthy, worthy, Worthy is the Lamb, The Lamb that was slain, Holy, holy, Jesus, I will sing, Sing of Your holy name

I love Thee because Thou hast first loved me, And purchased my pardon on Calvary's tree, I love Thee for wearing the thorns on Thy brow, If ever I loved Thee, my Jesus 'tis now

In mansions of glory and endless delight, I'll ever adore Thee in Heaven so bright, I'll sing with the glittering crown on my brow, If ever I loved Thee, My Jesus 'tis now

35
LOON OR SAINT?

I want this day to be a day that our stand and march for freedom for our children and grandchildren is strongly affirmed. It's not an easy place to stand in our shoes. Many of us are aware that others have deemed our faith for our children's freedom as foolish.

I believe you will echo my thoughts when I say; I'd rather be a fool in the eyes of the world and stand in faith in the eyes of my Creator Father. I'd rather be thought a loon, than embrace the diagnosis, thus making a mockery of the scars on my Savior's back in the eyes of my enemy.

Yes, we have chosen the road less traveled…actually I think we're still cutting down the trees as we go! Though this road is narrow, difficult and oft times lonely, take heart! Once you get home to Heaven, it will be too late to have faith. You won't stand in front of a 'Red Sea' in Heaven; it's only here on earth that we get to exercise our faith.

I realize that what I have written does not make your next hour radically different, but when you walk away from this book, when you walk into the next hour…though we cannot see each other…e are walking together. We are in this together and the God of Angel Armies goes with us, every step.

GOD SPEAKS:

"Be watchful, stand firm in the faith, act like men, be strong. Let all that you do be done in love." (1 Corinthians 16:13-14 ESV)

"Now who is there to harm you if you are zealous for what is good? But even if you should suffer for righteousness' sake, you will be blessed. Have no fear of them, nor be troubled, but in your hearts honor Christ the Lord as holy, always being prepared to make a defense to anyone who asks you for a reason for the hope that is in you; yet do it with gentleness and respect, having a good conscience, so that, when you are slandered, those who revile your good behavior in Christ may be put to shame. For it is better to suffer for doing good, if that should be God's will, than for doing evil." (1 Peter 3:13-17 ESV)

LET'S WORSHIP TOGETHER!

I Am Not Alone, Kari Jobe

When I walk through deep waters. I know that You will be with me.
When I'm standing in the fire. I will not be overcome. Through the
valley of the shadow

I will not fear. I am not alone. I am not alone. You will go before me.
You will never leave me.

In the midst of deep sorrow. I see Your light is breaking through . The
dark of night will not overtake me. I am pressing into You. Lord, You
fight my every battle. And I will not fear. You amaze me. Redeem me.

You call me as Your own. You're my strength. You're my defender.
You're my refuge in the storm. Through these trials. You've always been
faithful. You bring healing to my soul

36

LET'S REMEMBER TOGETHER!

Get your communion elements...we'll celebrate together today!

This is a great opportunity to remind ourselves why we believe what we believe! Let's take a close look at what the Word of God says about what Jesus did for our children concerning birth defect, which is by definition disease.

"Who has believed what he has heard from us? And to whom has the arm of the LORD been revealed? For he grew up before him like a young plant, and like a root out of dry ground; he had no form or majesty that we should look at him, and no beauty that we should desire him. He was despised and rejected by men; a man of sorrows, and acquainted with grief; and as one from whom men hide their faces, he was despised, and we esteemed him not. Surely he has borne (carried) our griefs (sickness & disease) and carried our sorrows; yet we esteemed him stricken, smitten by God, and afflicted. But he was pierced for our transgressions; he was crushed for our iniquities; upon him was the chastisement that brought us peace, and with his wounds we are healed.(heal, physician, cure, repaired) All we like sheep have gone astray; we have turned—every one—to his own way; and the LORD has laid on him the iniquity of us all. He was oppressed, and he was afflicted, yet he opened not his mouth; like a lamb that is led to the slaughter, and like a sheep that before its shearers is silent, so he opened not his mouth." (Isaiah 53:1-7 ESV)

Jesus paid the price in full for us to be right with the Father, joint heirs with Jesus Christ, and for our children to be healed in their bodies.

One day, when I was heavy in prayer with several other parents, I imagined Jesus as he stood at that whipping post on the way to the cross. I had the thought that maybe, just maybe, God let his son, Jesus, hear us, the parents, thanking him and praising him for healing our children. I imagined Jesus hearing our 'hallelujahs' and shouts of 'thanks' as he endured what must have been horrific pain and bodily trauma at that whipping post where our children's birth defects were carried in full.

As we break this bread, let's do it with loud 'hallelujahs' and praises to our King and Savior Jesus!

As we pour the cup, in remembrance of his blood shed for us, let us accept this place of right standing with our Father.

Together, with Jesus, we will march our children to the physical freedoms that were purchased with the flesh and blood of our King Jesus!

Hallelujah! Thank you Jesus!

GOD SPEAKS:

"He himself bore our sins in his body on the tree, that we might die to sin and live to" righteousness. By his wounds you have been healed. For you were straying like sheep, but have now returned to the Shepherd and Overseer of your souls." (1 Peter 2:24 ESV)

LET'S WORSHIP TOGETHER!

Revelation Song, Phillips, Craig & Dean

Worthy is the, Lamb who was slain, Holy, Holy, is He, Sing a new song, to Him who sits on, Heaven's Mercy Seat

Holy, Holy, Holy Is the Lord God Almighty Who was, and is, and is to come With all creation I sing: Praise to the King of Kings! You are my everything, And I will adore You...!

Clothed in rainbows, of living color. Flashes of lightning, rolls of thunder, Blessing and honor, strength and Glory and power be To You the Only Wise King, Yeah

Filled with wonder, Awestruck wonder, At the mention of Your Name, Jesus, Your Name is Power, Breath, and Living Water, Such a marvelous mystery Yeah...

Holy, Holy, Holy Is the Lord God Almighty Who was, and is, and is to come, With all creation I sing: Praise to the King of Kings! You are my everything, And – I - will - adore YOU...

Come up lift up His Name, To the King of Kings...We will adore YOU Lord...King of heaven and earth King Jesus, King Jesus Alleluia, alleluia, alleluia!

Majesty, awestruck Honor, And Power and Strength and Dominion To You Lord, To the King, to King To the King of Glory

37

"HOW YOU WAKE UP SETS YOUR DAY"

This morning as I got out of the bed (an *hour* after the alarm went off!), I heard these words roll around in my brain, "how you wake up sets your day".

I knew in my heart what that meant and it did *not* mean more coffee and a prayer. I knew that the way I faced the day would be a result of a determined mind and in turn produce success. I had lazily gotten out of the bed and probably would have slouched my way through the day had I not heard those words.

When we wake up and put our feet on the floor firmly, standing up straight and declaring the Word of the Lord…our day is set for success!

You know what I'm talking about, don't you?

I just moved 1700 miles to our new home and I am still in boxes. I could use some naps and even a vacation, but that is not in the plans. The reality is that I have children who need my attention, a husband who will come home from work wondering about supper, boxes to unpack, and laundry to be folded and put away. I need to be ministering healing to my child diagnosed with birth defect and I need to be 'attached to the vine' (John 15). You and I have busy days with priorities that probably no one else on the planet can attend to.

How we begin our day paves our path for success.

Here is my example on how to 'set' our day:

We hear our alarm clock and we roll out of the bed with a purposed smile and the determination of imminent victory for each hour of our day!

And out of our mouths flows a prophetic report of how things are going to be for the day:

'Thank you Father for this day! It is going to be a victorious day in the name of Jesus. I have wisdom and the mind of Christ. I have the energy and the focus to successfully accomplish everything that is before me this day. No weapon formed against my family or me will prosper in Jesus name. I have joy, I have focus, I have faith to move mountains and I have everything I need for life and Godliness. Powers of darkness you are bound in the name of Jesus and not permitted to produce fruit in my life nor in my children or husband's life.

My child is healed by the stripes of Jesus. Truth come forth in my child in Jesus name! Father, Jesus is Lord over this home. Your will is done on earth as it is in Heaven in this family. All opposition to the Father's will in this family is commanded to GO in the name of Jesus."

Thus a victorious day is launched from our forthright and determined attitude of waking up! One of the best parts of this is that we can do this together!

GOD SPEAKS:

"And if you are Christ's, then you are Abraham's offspring, heirs according to promise. "(Galatians 3:29 ESV)

"But you, Israel, my servant, Jacob, whom I have chosen, the offspring of Abraham, my friend; you whom I took from the ends of the earth, and called from its farthest corners, saying to you, "You are my servant, I have chosen you and not cast you off"; fear not, for I am with you; be not dismayed, for I am your God; I will strengthen you, I will help you, I will uphold you with my righteous right hand.

Behold, all who are incensed against you shall be put to shame and confounded; those who strive against you shall be as nothing and shall perish. You shall seek those who contend with you, but you shall not find them; those who war against you shall be as nothing at all. For I, the LORD your God, hold your right hand; it is I who say to you, "Fear not, I am the one who helps you." (Isaiah 41:8-13 ESV)

LET'S WORSHIP TOGETHER!
Christ Redeemer, Nate Marialke

Crown Him with many crowns, bow down before Him now Here is love and victory, reaching through the ages Reaching here to me Christ Redeemer, Christ our healer Christ the victor, servant King

Savior forever, mercy unending Lord eternal, Prince of Peace Creation at Your command, by nature the Great I am From highest heaven to manger bed, You took on human likeness

You crushed the serpents head When all the nations come, every kindred tribe and tongue Through every age, this anthem raise Jesus bought me, redeemed me with His blood Lord eternal, Prince of Peace

38

THE POWER OF WORDS

I did an experiment on the tangible power of our words about a year ago. I actually got the idea from a man who did a similar experiment and posted it on a YouTube video. He is not a Christian, but clearly understands the power of words.

Here is the experiment:

I took three mason jars and put equal amounts of raw rice in each jar.

I then covered the rice in the jars with water. I labeled the jars and spoke the three following statements to the jars once a day repeating the statement three times. One of my children actually did this experiment with me. One jar was the 'control' jar and was spoken nothing to. One jar was spoken to with these words: "you are sick". One jar was spoken to with these words: "by the stripes of Jesus, you are healed".

For one month, one time a day my five year old son and I spoke to the rice.

Within 24 hours two of the jars of rice were absorbing the water. One was not.

Within 24 hours the color of one jar in particular was visually different from the other two.

At the end of the experiment, each jar of rice was visually different from the other.

The jar that was spoken nothing to had absorbed all the water and also rotted, but it was more of a reddish color of rot as opposed to the greyish blackish rotting color of the 'you are sick' jar.

The jar that was spoken words of life to did not absorb the water and turned a unified brownish color.

How can this be?

If God said that there is power of life and death in our words, then that is the truth! If Jesus spoke to a fig tree and then told us to speak to mountains, then that is the truth! If the Word of God said we would eat the fruit of our mouth, then that is the truth! The Word of God is our final authority.

Man's experience, logic and reason should not dictate to us what our belief system should be. Our beliefs should rest solely on our Bible, our God's words to us.

When a child is born with an incurable disease, a birth defect, the parents have choices. We can let man's experience, logic and reason dictate to us how to deal with the diagnosis; OR we can go to the Book given to us by our God and see what He says we should do about the diagnosis.
Rest assured, the path you have chosen is a narrow one indeed, but we aren't the only ones in history to believe our God for the impossible. We aren't the only ones in history to believe the promises of God. We have what it takes to set our children free and we have each other to stand beside in faith.

Speak life. Speak words of life that are beautiful about your child, yourself, and your life today.

Let's not say anything that will produce the kind of fruit that we do not want in our children or our own lives. We'll do it together!

GOD SPEAKS:

"Death and life are in the power of the tongue, and those who love it will eat its fruits." (Proverbs 18:21,ESV)

LET'S WORSHIP TOGETHER!

'I will Exalt', Amanda Falk

Your Presence is all I need. It's all I want, all I seek . Without it, without it there's no meaning. Your Presence is the air I breathe.
The song I sing, the love I need .Without it, without it I'm not living
I will exalt You, Lord, I will exalt You, Lord. There is no one like You God.
I will exalt You, Lord, I will exalt You, Lord. No other name be lifted high There will be no one like You. And no one beside You. You alone are worthy of all praise.
There will be no one like You. And no one beside You. You alone are worthy of all praise

39

WE'RE IN GOOD COMPANY

How do you think Noah felt when he started to build that ark? I imagine that he was already experiencing separation from society before he cut down the trees for his houseboat! The Word of God says that he was righteous and that the grace of God was upon him. We share these two things in common with Noah. We have been made righteous by the blood of Jesus and God's grace is also upon our lives.

Imagine with me what it must have looked like when God closed the only exit to the ark.

There would have been lots of sounds and smells, no doubt. Noah, his wife, Noah's three sons and daughters-in-law were sitting in the ark for seven days before the first drop of rain fell.

By faith, Noah chopped the wood and built the ark. By faith, Noah entered the ark. By faith, he stayed in the ark for seven days with no sign of the promised rain.

By faith, we believe the Word of God. By faith, we speak to their bodies. By faith, we thank the Father for healing our children's bodies. By faith, we expect the truth to manifest. By faith, no matter what we see with our eyes or hear with our ears, we believe that God is faithful and will perform his word. By faith, we believe!

GOD SPEAKS:

'Trust in the LORD with all your heart and do not lean on your own understanding. In all your ways acknowledge him, and he will make straight your paths.' (Proverbs 3:5-6 ESV)

'Therefore, if anyone is in Christ, he is a new creation. The old has passed away; behold, the new has come. All this is from God, who through Christ reconciled us to himself and gave us the ministry of reconciliation; that is, in Christ God was reconciling the world to himself, not counting their trespasses against them, and entrusting to us the message of reconciliation. Therefore, we are ambassadors for Christ, God making his appeal through us. We implore you on behalf of Christ, be reconciled to God. For our sake he made him to be sin who knew no sin, so that in him we might become the righteousness of God.' (2 Corinthians 5:17-21 ESV)

LET'S WORSHIP TOGETHER!

Passion-Here's My Heart, Crowder

Here's my heart Lord, Here's my heart Lord Here's my heart Lord, Speak what is true

'Cause I am found, I am Yours, I am loved, I'm made pure, I have life, I can breathe, I am healed, I am free

(Chorus)

Here's my heart Lord, Here's my heart Lord, Here's my heart Lord, Speak what is true 'Cause I am found, I am Yours, I am loved, I'm made pure, I have life, I can breathe I am healed, I am free 'Cause You are strong, You are sure,

You are life, You endure, You are good, always true, You are light breaking through Here's my heart Lord, Here's my heart Lord, Here's my heart Lord, Speak what is true Here's my life Lord…

I am found, I am Yours. I am loved, I'm made pure. I have life, I can breathe. I am healed, I am free 'Cause You are strong, You are sure. You are life, You endure.

You are good, always true. You are light breaking through. You are more than enough. You are here, You are love. You are hope, You are grace. You're all I have, You're everything

40

THE NEXT TWENTY MINUTES

(I give to you what my dad gave to me, this 'one-
twenty minutes at a time' act of faith!)

This is a battle of faith. It is an epic battle because it involves
destinies, namely our children's. The church, as a whole,
appears to have left us on a battlefield that is isolated. This may
be the truth in the natural, but it is not that way in the spirit
realm. If our spiritual eyes were opened, I believe we would see
that, truly, there are more for us than against us, just like
Elisha's servant saw!

Take courage. You are not alone. Not only are other parents
standing on this same battlefield of faith, but there are angels all
around, harkening to the Word of God that comes forth from
our mouths.

How do we continue? One twenty minutes at a time! You only
have to be victorious for the next twenty minutes. Stand in
faith, speak the Word of God, take courage, think positive
thoughts, drink a cup of yum…and when this twenty minutes
of victory is at its end, then take charge of the next twenty
minutes; but do not think about the next hour, just be
victorious one twenty minutes at a time. We will do this
together and see our children completely free!

GOD SPEAKS:

'When the servant of the man of God rose early in the morning
and went out, behold, an army with horses and chariots was all
around the city. And the servant said, "Alas, my master! What
shall we do?" He said, "Do not be afraid, for those who are
with us are more than those who are with them." Then Elisha
prayed and said, "O LORD, please open his eyes that he may
see." So the LORD opened the eyes of the young man, and he
saw, and behold, the mountain was full of horses and chariots
of fire all around Elisha.' (2 Kings 6:15-17 ESV)

"Bless the LORD, O my soul, and all that is within me, bless
his holy name! Bless the LORD, O my soul, and forget not all
his benefits, who forgives all your iniquity, who heals all your
diseases, who redeems your life from the pit, who crowns you
with steadfast love and mercy, who satisfies you with good so
that your youth is renewed like the eagles. The LORD works
righteousness and justice for all who are oppressed. He made
known his ways to Moses, his acts to the people of Israel. The
LORD is merciful and gracious, slow to anger and abounding in
steadfast love. He will not always chide, nor will he keep his
anger forever. He does not deal with us according to our sins,
nor repay us according to our iniquities. For as high as the
heavens are above the earth, so great is his steadfast love
toward those who fear him; as far as the east is from the west,
so far does he remove our transgressions from us. As a father
shows compassion to his children, so the LORD shows
compassion to those who fear him. For he knows our frame; he
remembers that we are dust. As for man, his days are like grass;
he flourishes like a flower of the field; for the wind passes over
it, and it is gone, and its place knows it no more. But the
steadfast love of the LORD is from everlasting to everlasting
on those who fear him, and his righteousness to children's
children, to those who keep his covenant and remember to do
his commandments. The LORD has established his throne in
the heavens, and his kingdom rules over all. Bless the LORD,

O you his angels, you mighty ones who do his word, obeying the voice of his word! Bless the LORD, all his hosts, his ministers, who do his will! Bless the LORD, all his works, in all places of his dominion. Bless the LORD, O my soul!" (Psalm 103:1-22 ESV)

LET'S WORSHIP TOGETHER!

Let it be Jesus, Christy Nockels

The first name that I call. Let it be Jesus. My song inside the storm. I'll never need another...

For me to live is Christ. For me to live is Christ. God, I breathe Your name. Above everything Let it be, let it be Jesus. Let it be, let it be Jesus. Let it be Jesus.

From the rising of the sun. And let it be Jesus When all is said and done. I'll never need another. Jesus, there's no other...

Should I ever be abandoned, Should I ever be acclaimed, Should I ever be surrounded, By the fire and the flame,

There's name I will remember, There's a name I will proclaim Let it be, let it be Jesus. Let it be, let it be Jesus.

Let it be, let it be...

WORLD WHIPPING POST AWARENESS DAY

W.W.P.A.D.

WHEN: This day will be observed on November 17th from this time forth until the return of our Savior.

WHAT? World Whipping Post Awareness Day is designated for Christians around the world to call special honor of what our Savior Jesus Christ has done to set free those diagnosed with birth defects. As believers in Jesus Christ, we declare to the world, that our God and His words to us concerning bodily healing apply to those with birth defect and that our God is trustworthy and deserving of our faith.

HOW? We are asking all believers to observe World Whipping Post Awareness Day in order to raise public awareness of the finished and marvelous work of Jesus at the whipping post concerning birth defects.

Red will be the color of choice to wear on this special day in honor of the high price that was paid by King Jesus.

You can also use this as an opportunity to encourage believers to faith and action through the use of social media and by educating your church, prayer group, or Bible study. Promotional materials for this purpose will be available to make it easy for anyone to spread the word.[3]

---

[3] You will be able to find these promotional materials at FullSpeedImpact.com or the Full Speed Impact Facebook or Twitter pages.

However, the most honorable thing you could do in remembering and recognizing what Jesus has done at the whipping post would be to make a difference in those seeking complete freedom from genetic birth defects. On this day, let us reaffirm that persons with birth defects are entitled to the full and effective enjoyment of all human rights and fundamental freedoms granted to us all by Jesus. Let the believer do their part through understanding who they are In Christ Jesus and the power of the Holy Spirit and faith in Jesus Christ, to enable children and persons with birth defects to participate fully in the development and life of their societies on an equal basis with others. Believers will do this by not only observing the truth of the freedoms found through the work of Jesus, but also let the believers strengthen those who seek full recovery and perfection in their genetic makeup by standing in faith and the laying on of hands and declaring the will of God and Jesus in these said people as it is in heaven.

On this day, do something that will change destinies and fulfill the will of our God to celebrate what Jesus did with his life that day that will echo throughout history when he willingly stood at that whipping post and carried birth defects so children and adults alike would not have to. Don't simply pray for children born and diagnosed with birth defects on WWPAD, but make a commitment to walk the path of freedom with these children and their parents and grandparents until every chromosome in the children lines up with the Word and Work of Jesus at the whipping post!

WHY? World Whipping Post Awareness Day is a wakeup call to the Body of Christ and a notice that the suffering of Jesus Christ at the whipping post has provided us the power and authority to set the captives free from all diseases and genetic defects.

This day for World Whipping Post Awareness Day being the 17th day of the eleventh month was selected in honor of Erika Blake born on this day to Dawn and Curry Blake, general overseers of John G. Lake Ministries. The birth defect that Erika was born with sparked a quest of truth and knowledge in Biblical healing for her parents. Because of their quest, many have found freedom in bodily healing.

Let the believers stand in this committed manner until everyone who desires freedom from birth defects is 100% free. Let the believer be aware that the missing link to the healing of chromosomes is found in the body of Christ Jesus which is full of the resurrection power of God and present on earth.

RECOMMENDED RESOURCES

God Heals Birth Defects — First Fruits is a revolutionary book that will encourage, challenge, and equip you to minister healing in seemingly impossible situations. Written with a team of amazing parents from around the world, this book is packed with testimonies from parents who are seeing God heal their children afflicted with diagnosis such as autism, down syndrome, and cerebral palsy.

You will read of:

➤ Doctors amazed by disappearing defects

➤ Children moved to normal classes because they no longer qualify as "special needs"

➤ Organs, bones, facial features, and muscles restored to normal function

➤ Families restored to joy and peace by the truth of God's grace.

If you are looking for hope and practical Biblical answers that will empower you to minister healing to those afflicted with birth defects, and are ready to step into a lifestyle that truly manifests "All things are possible with God," this book is for you!

You will find additional books, study guides, and video resources from Andy Hayner at his ministry website, **FullSpeedImpact.com**.

If you want to learn how to experience the power of your identity in Christ, **Your Place in the Son** is the book for you. You will see the reality of your union with Jesus Christ like never before and learn how to break free from negative emotions and carnal mindsets to walk in the freedom, joy, and power of the Spirit of God. Reading this book will absolutely transform your walk with God and 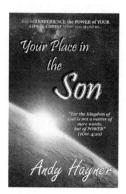 show you how to walk in the victory and love of Jesus Christ.

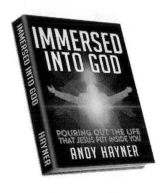 Andy's book, **Immersed into God**, and the **Immersed into God Interactive Training Manual** will equip you to experience your identity in Christ and to walk in His power to impact the world around you! Filled with examples, Biblical insights, and practical coaching, you will learn to experience God's power in your own life and learn a variety of ways to release His power to others— healing the sick, prophetic evangelism, ministering the baptism of the Holy Spirit, deliverance and casting out demons, making friends with strangers, and establishing disciples of Jesus Christ who walk in His supernatural power.

Andy's book, **Born to Heal** and the **Born to Heal Interactive Training Manual** is packed with testimonies, Scripture, frequently asked questions and proven training that will revolutionize your life! If you are looking for a book that will equip you with a solid Biblical and practical foundation that will empower you to heal the sick as a lifestyle, this is it! Never again will you feel helpless in the face of sickness!

SPIRIT CRY- of a Child of God in the Embrace of the Father! The best way to accelerate your spiritual transformation is by learning how to tap into your identity in the Spirit. This book shows you how!

Tara Ashworth contributed many of the "Let's Worship Together" sections of this book. She is a worship leader in Canada who not only leads worship in her city, but also leads an organized global worship ministry for Team Avalanche. She and her husband, Wade, are also parents who are speaking Life and declaring the finished work of Christ over their own children. If you are interested in having them minister in your city, please contact them at tashworth597@gmail.com .

ABOUT THE AUTHOR

Margaret Weishuhn is the founder of Team Avalanche, a global ministry dedicated to mobilizing the church to heal birth defects in Jesus' name. She is also the leader of a John G. Lake Ministry Life Team comprised of parents ministering healing to their own children diagnosed with birth defects. Margaret is one of a multitude of parents scattered throughout the earth who are standing on the promises of God for the healing of their children diagnosed with birth defect. She leads a global team of parents who have decided to take God at His word, in spite of the universal mindset regarding birth defects — a true global healing revival in its genesis. Margaret is a voice in this sea of parents whose recorded words will testify to a good and faithful God whose name is Jehovah Rapha, the "The Lord That Heals". She and her husband have been married for twenty-five years and have five children.

Made in the USA
Middletown, DE
27 July 2018